To my children Benyamin, Nathalie, and Dan.

May you embody your full sovereignty and radiate your own light within this new paradigm.

CONSCIOUS VIBRATIONAL TRANSITION

TRANSFORMATION GUIDE

VIBRATIONAL CONSCIOUSNESS

INTUITIVE FREQUENCY THERAPY

MASTERY OF BODY AND SENSING

PRACTICAL ENERGY GUIDE

Theoretical and structural pillars, practical applications, and tools

By Yaacov Raanan – 2026 Edition

Paperback – US Trade (6 x 9 in/152 x 219 mm)

ISBN : 9782714909947

raananediteur. com

CONSCIOUS VIBRATIONAL TRANSITION

- **A6:** Digestion / Digestive Disorders
- **A7:** Stomach Pain
- **A8:** Back Care / Back Pain
- **A9:** Sleep Disorders
- **A10:** Quitting Smoking
- **A11:** Addictions – Drugs
- **A12:** Weight Loss
- **A13:** Immune System Strengthening
- **A14:** Vibrational Detox of the Physical Body

B. Emotional Protocols

- **B15:** Releasing Stress – Anxiety – Nervous Tension
- **B16:** Emotional Blockages – Grief – Shock
- **B17:** General Emotional Harmonization
- **B18:** Releasing Limiting Beliefs (Dissolving hurdles and re-installing positive alignment)
- **B19:** Releasing Emotional Shocks (Recent or old traumatic imprints)
- **B20:** Healing Repetitive Patterns (Transmuting negative cycles)
- **B21:** Reconnection / Awakening Joy and Serenity

C. Energetic Protocols

- **C22:** REALIGNMENT: Chakras + Aura + Meridians
- **C23:** Full Body-Soul-Spirit Harmonization
- **C24:** Full Chakra Care Protocol
- **C25:** Purification of Family Karma (Lineage and karmic memories)
- **C26:** Rebalancing Polarities (Yin/Yang)
- **C27:** Subconscious Cleaning (Releasing fears and programming)
- **C28:** Aura Cleaning
- **C29:** Activation of the 12 DNA Strands
- **C30:** Transgenerational Cleaning
- **C31:** Vibrational Field Harmonization
- **C32:** Vibrational Rate Dynamization
- **C33:** Cleaning Energetic Implants (Removing limiting programming/manipulations)
- **C34:** Matrix Realignment Care
- **C35:** Conscious Vibrational Protection
- **C36:** Deep Energetic Recharging

INTRODUCTION
THE PATH OF VIBRATIONAL CONSCIOUSNESS

1. The shift from the old to the new paradigm

We are leaving an era of density to enter the era of frequency. The old paradigm taught us that the body was an isolated biological machine, that disease was a mechanical fatality, and that the mind was merely a byproduct of the brain. In this vision, to act upon the living, an external tool was required: a machine, a plant, medicine, or even a pendulum.

The new paradigm proposed by **Conscious Vibrational Transition** reverses this perspective entirely. We are not solid beings living in a material world, but rather information systems in constant vibration. Here, consciousness is no longer a spectator; it is the conductor of the orchestra. To understand this paradigm is to realize that modifying one's frequency means modifying one's biological and emotional reality. This is no longer a mere belief; it is a moment-to-moment experience.

2. Why "Transition"? The art of shifting from state A to state B

The word "Transition" was chosen for its inherent dynamics. Nothing is static. Life is a perpetual movement between different vibrational states.

- **State A** represents your starting point: fatigue, emotional blockage, mental confusion, or physical pain. It is a low-frequency state where information flows poorly.
- **State B** is the state of fluidity, clarity, and vitality.

Transition is not a magical leap; it is a conscious process. It is the art of modulating one's own field so that energy no longer stagnates. In this training, you will learn that moving from A to B does not require force, but rather a fine-tuned intention and a total presence. You become the one who knows how to guide the flow back to where it had stopped.

3. The body as the sole instrument (The tool-free approach)

Herein lies the radical nature of this method: **you are the tool.**

We have been conditioned to seek external crutches (crystals, symbols, instruments). While these tools can assist, they often create dependency. Conscious Vibrational Transition bets on the power of the human instrument.

Your nervous system, your hands, your fascia, and your heart are receivers and transmitters of infinite precision. By developing your vibrational sensing, you learn to:

- Read information without any intermediary.
- Detect tissue resistance through simple proximity.
- Emit a corrective frequency through the mere coherence of your presence.

The "tool-free" approach guarantees total autonomy. Anywhere, at any time, you have your capacity for intervention at your disposal.

4. Reader commitment: from theory to inner sensing

This book is not a metaphysical treatise to be read for the accumulation of knowledge. It is a training manual. Theory is only present to reassure your mind and provide it with a framework for understanding. However, true knowledge will be born within your cells.

Your commitment is as follows: **Every chapter must be felt before it is validated**. If I speak of "recentering," do not be satisfied with merely understanding the concept; practice it until your body gives you the physical signal of change (heat, a sigh, a release).

To become a practitioner of Transition, you must agree to feel—moving from your head to your pelvis, from analysis to inner sensing. We are going to transform your perception so that you no longer "think" energy, but rather "live" it.

PART I: THE PILLARS OF THE UNITY OF LIFE

CHAPTER 1
UNDERSTANDING VIBRATIONAL NATURE

Welcome to the study of the foundation of all existence. Before we can transform or transmute a state, we must understand the matter of which we are made. In this chapter, we will deconstruct the material vision of the world to enter the reality of frequencies.

1. Energy, Frequency, and Vibration: Essential Nuances

In everyday language, we often use these terms as synonyms. However, for the Vibrational Transition practitioner, they describe three distinct and complementary aspects of reality.

- **Energy: The Fuel (The "Engine")**

  Energy is the capacity to act, the potential for movement. It is raw force. Imagine the water behind a dam: it is there, available, charged with power. In the human body, this is your global vitality, your "reservoir."

- **Vibration: The Movement (The "Breath")**

  Vibration is the setting in motion of this energy. Nothing is at rest. Your cells, your emotions, your thoughts are all oscillations. It is the swaying that gives shape to life. If energy is the water, vibration is the wave traveling across the surface of the lake.

- **Frequency: The Signature (The "Musical Note")**

  This is the measurement of the vibration (the number of oscillations per second). Here lies the key to the Transition.

  A low frequency corresponds to states of density, heaviness, disease, or fear.

  A high frequency corresponds to states of fluidity, joy, health, and clarity.

The core point of the training: In Vibrational Transition, we do not only seek to have "more energy"; we seek to modify the frequency to change the quality of the information circulating in the body.

2. The Unity of Life: Definition and Operational Mechanism

The Unity of Life (UL) is the central concept of this method. It represents the global balance of your energetic system at any given moment.

Definition:

The Unity of Life is the measurement of your vibrational coherence. It represents not only your physical health but the alignment between what you vibrate (your emotions), what you inform (your thoughts), and what you manifest (your body).

The Operational Mechanism:

Your Unity of Life functions like an intelligent, rechargeable battery:

- **Leaks**: Stress, parasitic thoughts, toxic environments, unsuitable diet. Every leak causes your UL to drop.

- **Self-Preservation**: The individual's ability to maintain their UL at a threshold level to remain sovereign over their health.
- **Recovery**: Through recentering and conscious breathing, we can instantly raise our UL level.

The practitioner's goal: To lead the client (or oneself) to stabilize their Unity of Life beyond external fluctuations. This is the transition from survival to conscious living.

3. The Law of Resonance: How Information Shapes Our Reality

We do not attract what we want; we attract what we vibrate. This is the Law of Resonance.

Information Primes Over Energy:

Energy is blind. It is information (your inner state, your memories, your intention) that directs it. Imagine a radio station: the wave is the energy, but the music you hear is the information.

- If your body "broadcasts" on the frequency of "lack" or "anger," it will resonate with all situations of the same frequency in your environment.

The Impact on Reality:

- **At the biological** level: An information of fear transmitted repeatedly eventually crystallizes matter and creates a tissue blockage (pain, tension).
- **At the relational** level: We pick up the vibrational fields of others. Resonance explains why certain presences instantly exhaust or inspire us.

Practical Application:

As a practitioner, you will learn to use your own field to create a healing resonance. By stabilizing your frequency in a state of "coherent neutrality," you allow the client's body—through simple vibrational proximity—to align with this health frequency. This is known as **frequency entrainment.**

SUMMARY FOR YOUR PRACTICE JOURNAL:

- **Energy = Quantity / Frequency = Quality.**
- **Unity of Life = My global coherence barometer.**
- **Resonance = I capture and emit what resembles me vibrationally.**

Transition note to the next chapter: Now that we understand the nature of the flow, how do we ensure we always remain at the center of our own axis? This is what we will discover with the mechanism of Recentering

TRAINING EXERCISE: The Inner Resonance Scale

Objective: Learn to estimate your percentage of Unity of Life (UL) autonomously and sensorially, without external tools.

In Vibrational Transition, we do not use external dowsing charts. We use our own nervous system as a cursor. This exercise will teach you to "calibrate" your sensing.

Step 1: Availability Scan

Sit quietly. Close your eyes. Take three deep breaths to clear surface tensions. Ask yourself internally, as if questioning every cell in your body:

"At what level is my global vitality right here and now?"

Step 2: Evaluation of the 3 Poles

To refine your measurement, review the three components of your UL:

- **The Physical Pole**: Do you feel heaviness or lightness in your limbs? Are your eyes tired?
- **The Emotional Pole**: What is the "color" of your inner weather? Is it calm, agitated, gray, or bright?
- **The Mental Pole**: Are your thoughts like a saturated radio or like a peaceful lake?

Step 3: Quantification (The Reflex-Number)

Do not think. Let a number between 0 and 100 rise to your mind. This is your "Reflex-Number." To validate this number, use the following correspondence table:

Estimated UL	Vibrational State	Bodily Signals / Types
85% - 100%	Full Coherence	Sensation of tingling, desire to create, clear vision, light body.
70% - 85%	Stable Balance	Calm, presence, ability to listen, healthy fatigue at end of day.
50% - 70%	Leakage Zone	Impatience, need for stimulants (coffee, sugar), circular thoughts.
Below 50%	Alert / Survival	Irritability, physical pain, "brain fog" sensation, exhaustion.

APPLICATION (Deep Reflection)

Learning to measure one's UL is putting an end to biological ignorance. Most people only realize they are at 30% UL when they fall ill or burn out.

The practitioner monitors their UL like a pilot monitors a dashboard. If the needle drops to 60%, they do not push through: they stop, recenter, and re-inform their field.

YOUR FIRST PRACTITIONER ASSIGNMENT

During the next 24 hours, note your UL level at three key moments:

1. **Upon waking**: What is your initial charge?
2. **After work**: What was the impact of your environment?
3. **Before sleeping**: In what state are you returning your energy to the night?

   Record these numbers in your logbook. You will begin to see the map of your own vibrational geography.

4. The Structure of the Unity of Life: The Three Currents Model

To properly pilot one's UL, the practitioner must understand that this battery is powered by three distinct, intersecting currents.

- **The Telluric Current (The Base Charge)**: This is Earth energy, raw physical vitality. It rises through the feet and nourishes the bone and muscle structure.

- **The Emotional Current (The Relationship Flow)**: This is the energy circulating between us and others. It settles in the center of the body.
- **The Informational Current (The Signal of Consciousness)**: This is the energy descending from the top of the head. It provides coherence to the whole.

During a session, you must identify which of these three currents is weakened to restore the client's global Unity of Life.

5. Entropy vs. Vibrational Negentropy

In the universe, two forces compete: entropy (disorder, degradation) and negentropy (organization, life).

- **Vibrational Entropy**: The state of a person whose UL is constantly dropping. They are subject to external frequencies and fragment.
- **Negentropy (The Transition)**: The action of the practitioner. Through intention and alignment, they reintroduce order and coherent information into the system.

6. Operational Synthesis: The 3 Golden Rules of Chapter 1

1. **Rule of Preservation**: "I can only transmit the frequency that I embody." (If you are stressed, you transmit stress).
2. **Rule of Resonance**: "Every physical blockage is a reflection of crystallized information." (The body never lies about the state of the UL).
3. **Rule of Transition**: "To change the frequency is to change the reality." (We do not fight the shadow; we increase the power of the light).

CONCLUSION OF CHAPTER 1

Understanding vibrational nature means ceasing to see yourself as a victim of circumstances to become a conscious modulator. You are no longer a solid object suffering the shocks of the world, but a symphony in constant rewriting. Your Unity of Life is your most precious asset. Tune it every day, for it is through it that you will perceive and transform the fabric of existence.

CHAPTER 2
RECENTERING – YOUR INNER COMPASS

Recentering is not a simple relaxation technique; it is the fundamental act of Vibrational Transition. In this chapter, we will discover how to bring all our power back into our axis to stop being subject to external influences.

1. The Vibrational and Neuronal Mechanism of Returning to Self

From a physiological and energetic standpoint, "Recentering" is the transition from a state of dispersion to a state of coherence.

- **On the neuronal level**: When we are decentered, our nervous system is in "alert" mode (sympathetic). The neocortex is saturated with thousands of pieces of information. Recentering means sending a signal to the vagus nerve to switch to parasympathetic mode. Brain chemistry changes: cortisol drops, oxytocin increases. You exit "survival" mode to enter "presence" mode.
- **On the vibrational level**: Imagine your energy field is like a bubble. When you are distracted, worried, or focused on someone else, your "energetic center of gravity" exits your physical body. You are literally "disconnected." Recentering is the magnetic action that draws all your particles of attention back to your central channel (the vertical axis). This is where your vibrational signature is at its purest and strongest.

2. Why Do We Flee? (Energetic Leaks)

The majority of individuals live in a state of constant flight without even realizing it. An "energetic leak" is a depletion of your Unity of Life.

- **Leakage through the mind**: It is the incessant travel between regrets of the past and anxiety about the future. Each non-productive thought is a breach through which your energy escapes.
- **Leakage through unmastered empathy**: Projecting yourself into another person's field to try to understand or save them. By doing this, you drain your own reservoir.
- **External stimuli**: Screens, noises, artificial emergencies. Modern society is designed to "extract" us from ourselves.

We learn this: One cannot perform a Vibrational Transition on others if one is in a state of flight themselves. Recentering is the first act of sovereignty. It is deciding that, for this moment, nothing is more important than the presence within ourselves.

3. Protocol: The Immediate Recentering Exercise

This is the basic tool you will use before every session, every important decision, or as soon as you feel overwhelmed.

Objective: Bring energy back to the axis in less than 3 minutes.

1. **The Posture of the Axis**: Sit with your feet flat or remain standing. Feel the weight of your body. Release your jaw (the mental lock).

2. **The Call-to-Self Breath**: Inhale deeply through the nose, imagining you are drawing back all your attention scattered outside. Exhale through the mouth, letting this attention descend and settle into your pelvis (your center of gravity).
3. **Activation of the Zero Point**: Bring your consciousness to the center of your chest, then descend three centimeters behind the sternum. This is your anchor point. Visualize a dense, fixed point of light.
4. **Vibrational Affirmation**: Pronounce internally (or aloud): "I return to my Center. I am here and now. I reclaim all my energy."
5. **Sensing the Contour**: Regain awareness of your boundaries. Feel the density of your presence. You no longer "think," you "are."

TRAINING ADVICE: Practice this protocol 10 times a day, in short 30-second sequences. The goal is to create a "vibrational reflex." The more often you recenter, the more your body will recognize this path and settle into it permanently. A recentered practitioner is a practitioner whose simple field of presence is sometimes enough to soothe the client.

4. The Physiology of Recentering: What Happens in Your Cells

Recentering is not just a mental exercise; it is a measurable biological change. When you bring your attention back inside your axis, you trigger a cascade of reactions:

- **Electrical Calm**: Your brainwave activity slows down. You shift from Beta waves (agitation, analysis) to Alpha waves (vigilant relaxation). It is in this state that your vibrational "antenna" becomes most precise.
- **Natural Heart Coherence**: By bringing your consciousness to the Zero Point (behind the sternum), your heart rate regulates itself. This regularity creates a powerful and stable magnetic field that begins to radiate around you.
- **Micro-Tissue Relaxation**: Your fascia (the tissues surrounding your organs and muscles) release. This relaxation is the sine qua non condition for energy to circulate again without obstacle.

5. Recentering in Action

In your practice, you will encounter two types of recentering: Preparatory Recentering and Maintenance Recentering.

1. **Preparatory Recentering** (Before the session): Total immersion. You take the time to verify every level of your axis.
2. **Maintenance Recentering (During the session)**: The ability to return to yourself while remaining in interaction with the client. The Trap: Letting yourself be "sucked in" by the client's pain or story. Correction: If you feel you are losing your axis, exhale deeply and regain support through your heels.

6. ADVANCED EXERCISE: Dynamic Recentering (The Movement Test)

This exercise is designed to test the solidity of your axis in real life.

- **Static Phase**: Perform your usual recentering protocol. Feel your solidity.
- **Movement Phase**: Start walking slowly around the room, keeping 80% of your attention fixed on your Zero Point (your center).
- **Disturbance Phase**: Turn on the radio, a bright light, or ask someone to talk to you. The goal: Maintain the sensation of your axis despite external solicitations. If you feel your attention drifting, gently pull it back to your center.

7. SUMMARY FOR YOUR PRACTICE JOURNAL

Recentering is the transition from reaction to response.

- A decentered person reacts to the frequencies of others (they get angry, exhausted, anxious).
- A recentered person responds from their own frequency.

  Transition Key: The practitioner's strength does not lie in the ability to "send" energy, but in the ability to not leave their center.

8. Obstacles to Recentering: Identifying "Presence Thieves"

- **Mental Parasitism (The "Crazy Monkey")**: Automatic thoughts arising as soon as you close your eyes. Solution: Stay focused on the physical sensation of your weight on the chair.
- **Vibrational Impatience**: Wanting to "feel" something immediately. Solution: Return to "Neutral Observation" mode.
- **Residual Emotional Charge**: An event from the day "sticking" to your field. Solution: Use the Cleaning Breath. Exhale powerfully, visualizing gray smoke being evacuated.

9. The "Zero Point" State: The Gateway to Transition

Recentering leads to what we call the Zero Point. It is a state of active emptiness.

- **Definition**: The precise moment where you are no longer in the past, future, judgment, or desire. You are simply a conscious "witness."
- **Why is it crucial?** It is only from the Zero Point that the Law of Resonance functions purely. If you are not at the Zero Point, you transmit your own doubts or tensions to the client.

10. OPERATIONAL SYNTHESIS: The Sovereignty Routine

- **Morning (Calibration)**: 2 minutes of recentering upon waking.
- **Noon (Recovery)**: 1 minute of recentering before eating.
- **Evening (Release):** 3 minutes of recentering followed by disconnection.

CONCLUSION OF CHAPTER 2

Recentering is the greatest gift you can give yourself. It is the end of internal exile. By returning to the center, you discover that you possess a source of unalterable stability, regardless of the world's agitation. Once this center is established, we can now learn to anchor it so it becomes your unshakable foundation.

CHAPTER 3
GROUNDING AND THE VERTICAL AXIS

(This section explores the mechanics of grounding, not as a mere mental image, but as a physiological and vibrational connection to the Earth pole.)

If recentering (Chapter 2) consists of bringing one's scattered parts back to the center, grounding is the step that allows this presence to stabilize over time. Without grounding, the practitioner is like an antenna without a ground wire: they capture everything but eventually become saturated or toppled by the slightest environmental storm.

1. Body-Soul-Spirit Alignment: Sacred Verticality

Alignment is not an abstract concept; it is a structural reality of the Vibrational Being. Imagine a channel of light passing through the top of your skull, descending along the spine, and sinking into the ground.

- **The Body (The Temple)**: The material base, the receptacle. Without an inhabited body, energy cannot incarnate. Alignment begins with the physical sensation of one's supports.
- **The Soul (The Breath)**: The intermediary, the seat of your emotions and deep intuition. It gives color and direction to the energy.
- **The Spirit (The Consciousness)**: The superior pole, pure intelligence, and intention.

In training mode: "Vertical" alignment is verified by the feeling of a "just" tension (neither too soft nor too rigid). When these three poles are aligned on the same axis, the body's electrical resistance decreases, allowing the "Vibrational Transition" to operate with maximum efficiency and minimum effort.

2. Maintaining a High Energy Reservoir Against the Environment

Living in awareness means understanding that we bathe in an ocean of frequencies (noise, others' stress, electromagnetic waves). The challenge is not to cut oneself off from the world, but to maintain one's Unity of Life at a level higher than that of the environment.

- **The Law of Communicating Vessels**: If your vibrational rate is low, you will absorb surrounding "pollutions." If your reservoir is full and your frequency is high, your environment will adjust to you.
- **Positive Saturation:** Maintaining a high reservoir consists of saturating your cells with your own presence. A space occupied by your consciousness cannot be "squatted" by another's energy.
- **Nutrition and Rhythms**: This book emphasizes the importance of nourishing the physical body (pure water, living food) so that the energy support remains conductive.

3. Daily Vibrational Self-Preservation

Self-preservation is not "protection" in a defensive sense (as erecting walls also blocks good energies), but rather sovereignty.

- **The Coherence Bubble**: Learn to define your vital space. It is not a barrier, but a zone of influence where you decide which frequency dominates.
- **Conscious Disconnection**: Knowing how to withdraw your energetic "filaments" from situations or people that drain your Unity of Life.
- **The Tree Reflex**: At any time of the day, visualize roots extending from your feet and perineum. Feel excess mental charge being evacuated into the earth, while the earth's stability rises within you.

4. Protocol: Conscious Verticality – The Pillar of Light

Exercise: "The Pillar of Light"

1. **Feet**: Spread them to hip-width. Unlock the knees.
2. **Pelvis**: Imagine your sacrum is a heavy weight pulling your spine downward.
3. **Crown**: Imagine a silk thread pulling the top of your skull toward the sky.
4. **Breathing**: Inhale from the earth to the heart; exhale from the heart to the sky. Then reverse.
5. **Sensing**: Feel this stretch between the top and bottom. You are no longer a mass of flesh; you are a channel of transmission.

5. Managing the Energy Reservoir Against the Environment

As a conscious practitioner, you must understand that your Unity of Life (UL) is not a closed circuit; it constantly interacts with the places and people you encounter.

- **The Law of Vibrational Osmosis**: Naturally, energy flows from "fuller" to "emptier." If you enter a room charged with sadness with a low UL, you will absorb that sadness by osmosis.
- **Positive Saturation**: The best defense is not isolation, but saturation. Imagine a sponge already soaked in pure water: it can no longer absorb vinegar. By maintaining your energy through grounding, you saturate your cells with your own vibrational signature.
- **The Safety Threshold**: In training mode, we learn never to begin a session if our own UL is below 70%. Below this, you are no longer transmitting; you are compensating, which leads to exhaustion.

6. Self-Preservation: From the "Bubble" to "Radiance"

- **The Trap of the Bubble**: Visualizing a protective shell can create separation and fear. Furthermore, a bubble eventually depletes if not powered.
- **Radiance**: Since you are grounded (connected to Earth) and aligned (connected to Heaven), you have access to an infinite energy source. Instead of enclosing yourself, let this energy overflow from your axis and radiate 360 degrees around you.
- **The Presence Effect**: This radiance creates a zone of coherence. You become a "lighthouse": the lighthouse does not fight the darkness; it simply shines.

7. CLOSING EXERCISE: Sealing the Axis

Objective: To fix your grounding for several hours.

1. **Rooting**: Visualize your roots sinking to the center of the earth.
2. **The Column of Light**: Inhale this telluric force up your spine to the crown.
3. **Expansion**: On the exhale, imagine this light descending and enveloping your body like a cloak of presence.
4. **The Decree of Sovereignty**: Say mentally: "I am grounded, I am aligned, I am sovereign. Nothing that does not belong to me can attach to my field."

SUMMARY FOR YOUR PRACTICE JOURNAL:

Grounding and the vertical axis transform the practitioner into a **Mediator**.

- Without grounding, you are a dreamer.
- Without an axis, you are a follower.
- With both, you become the bridge through which healing information can descend into matter.

ADVICE:

Grounding is the secret of great magnetizers. An ill-grounded practitioner ends their day exhausted. A perfectly grounded practitioner ends their sessions more energized than at the start, having served as a fluid channel between Heaven and Earth without using their own survival reserves.

Note of Transition: Your foundations are now solid. In Part II, we will learn to use this stability to become a "detector" and learn to read vibrational information in others.

CHAPTER 4
DEVELOPING INTUITION & THE VIBRATIONAL MIND

Intuition is not a gift reserved for a few. It is a natural function, integrated into your vibrational system, as real as breathing or digestion. It acts constantly, but in most people, it is stifled by mental noise, emotional overload, hyper-stimulation, or ancient fears.

In this chapter, you will learn to awaken, stabilize, and direct your intuition. You will also discover the concept of the vibrational mind, a form of higher intelligence —finer, faster, and more aligned than the ordinary mind. This chapter moves you from "I sometimes perceive" to "I read energy naturally."

1. Passive Intuition vs. Active Intuition

There are two major families of intuition. Understanding them changes everything in vibrational practice.

1. **Passive Intuition**

- This is "spontaneous" intuition, appearing:
- In a calm moment, a conversation, or a dream.
- During meditation or a moment of letting go.
- It arrives on its own, like an obvious fact. It requires no effort. Limit: It does not always appear when you need it.

2. **Active Intuition**

- This is intuition triggered voluntarily by a change in one's internal state. It requires:
- Recentering and lowering mental activity.
- Directed attention and conscious breathing.
- Emotional neutrality.
- This intuition is the heart of vibrational reading. It is what practitioners and energy workers use. This chapter teaches you to enter this mode at will.

2. Intuitive Reading of Situations

Reading a situation intuitively means perceiving the energy of a place, a relationship, a project, or a decision.

1. **The Principle**: Every situation has a frequency. A choice has an energetic direction. When you ask, "Is this right for me?" it is not a mental analysis; it is a vibrational reading.
2. **How to read intuitively**:
    - **Neutral State**: Breath, alignment, presence.
    - **Connect**: Without mentalizing, just feel the situation.
    - **Observe**: The internal reaction is the message (Expansion = Good sign / Contraction = Warning).
    - **Trust:** The first impression is almost always the correct one.

3. Vibrational Sensory Development

Intuition develops through the subtle senses, which are identical to physical senses but applied to the vibrational plane:

- **Clair-sentience**: The body recognizes truth (heat/cold, density/lightness). This is the base of vibrational diagnosis.
- **Clair-cognizance**: You simply "know" without knowing how.
- **Clair-information**: Receiving a complete data set (e.g., "diaphragm tension," "mental overload").
- **Clair-voyance**: Often symbolic or metaphorical images (rather than "seeing things in the air").

4. The "Present Moment" Technique

A direct entry point into active intuition based on three axes:

- **Instant Breath**: A slow inhale/conscious exhale to lower mental noise.
- **Suspension of Commentary**: Observing without internal labeling for just one second.
- **Fine Attention**: Placing focus on the specific question or zone.

5. Intuitive Expansion

Once in an intuitive state, you can "widen" your perception, like increasing the brightness of your internal system.

- **Exercise**: Breathe slowly, feel the space around you like a halo, and let that halo grow.
- **What it reveals**: Emotional tensions in a place, the coherence of a project, or subtle information in a situation. It is the "flashlight" of your vibrational field.

6. High-Frequency Mind

The mind is not the enemy; it only becomes a problem when it is too loud or controlling.

A **high-frequency mind** is:

- Clear, soft, and silent.
- Solution-oriented and synchronized with intuition.

  To activate it: Use low breathing, grounding, and an intention that lets go of the specific answer.

7. EXERCISE: The Parabola (Accelerated Energetic Capture)

An advanced exercise to capture information instantly by bypassing the analytical mind.

- **Objective**: Capture vibrational data before the mind can interpret it.
- **The Steps**:
  1. **Contact Point**: Place your hand (or attention) on the zone or question.
  2. **Instant Silence**: Turn off internal speech for just one second.

3. **The Rebound**: Let the info "bounce" from the zone, through your field, and into your mental space.
4. **Reception**: Take the very first image, sensation, or word that arrives.

- **Why it works**: The mind doesn't have time to interpret. The information arrives raw and intact.

CONCLUSION OF CHAPTER 4

You now have the foundations to function in a stable intuitive mode. Whether for diagnosis, personal decisions, or daily life, you can now access active intuition, vibrational sensing, and the high-frequency mind.

PART II: EXPLORING THE BODY-AS-INSTRUMENT

CHAPTER 5
ENERGETIC READING & VIBRATIONAL DIAGNOSIS

Reading energy means learning to perceive what is invisible to the naked eye but influences every second of life: internal movement, flows, saturated zones, vibrational colors, rhythms of the subtle body, the circulation of the emotional system, mental charges, and even memories stored within physical matter.

This chapter opens the doors to **vibrational diagnosis**, an art that blends perception, intuition, structure, technique, and deep listening. We will move from the why to the how, and above all, how to apply it.

1. How to "See" Vibrationally

Vibrational vision is not necessarily visual. It can be for some, but it is not the rule. Instead, it manifests as a **subtle multi-sensory perception**, a set of internal signals.

1. **The 3 Main Types of Vibrational Vision**

- **Perceptive Vision**: The body feels before the mind understands (chills, thermal variations, tingling, pressure, lightness/density).
- **Intuitive Vision**: A form of information that "drops in," a knowing without reflection. This is the most natural path.
- **Semi-Visual Vision**: Some see colors, flows, or opaque zones. This is not the goal; it is simply one possible modality.

2. **The Fundamental Principle: Energy Reacts to Your Attention**

- You do not "see" energy as something external. You **feel how your own field reacts to the field of the other** (or your own). It is a vibrational dialogue—one nervous system meeting another.

2. Visual, Intuitive, and Corporeal Reading

Energetic reading is divided into three main axes. You can use one or combine all three.

1. **Visual Reading**

- Here, we observe the physical body to read the subtle body. We look at:
- Posture and micro-asymmetries.
- Frozen zones or internally rotated shoulders.
- High/low breathing and the speed of eye blinking.
- Grounding/footing on the floor.
- Example: A slightly raised shoulder = mental overload + old emotional tension.

2. **Intuitive Reading**

- You receive information "in blocks": "there is a weight at the plexus," "old stress in the lower back," "the mind is saturated." You do not search; you allow it to emerge in stillness.

3. **Corporeal Reading (By Hand)**

- This is the most reliable: the body never lies. Pass your hands 5–15 cm from the body, slowly, with soft attention.
- Feel for: Density, heat, cold, stagnation, pulsation, emptiness, or resistance. Each sensation is a piece of information.

3. Express Vibrational Test

A quick mini-reading to identify which zones need work in seconds.

1. **Presence**: Enter a neutral state with conscious breathing.
2. **Focus**: Place your attention on the person (or yourself).
3. **Internal Inquiry**: Ask, "Show me the most charged zone."
4. **Observe the signal**: An image, a tension in your own body, an involuntary hand movement, a hot spot, or an internal "call."

   This takes literally 3 to 8 seconds.

4. Detecting Zones to Relieve

1. **Signals of a Charged Zone**: Subtle hardness, "vibrational wall" sensation, excessive heat, deep cold, "sucking vacuum," irregular mini-pulsations, or a zone that "repels" the hand.
2. **Signals of a Weakened Zone**: Soft zone, absence of vibrational response, impression of "gray" or "faint," diffused cold, almost absent local breathing. These zones need recharging, not clearing.

5. Distance Evaluation

Distance evaluation is simple if you respect 3 criteria:

1. **Precise Mental Image**: Imagine the person is in front of you; your field will synchronize.
2. **Targeted Intention**: Connect to a specific point ("show me the plexus").
3. **Absolute Neutrality**: Do not project; only observe.

   Distance reading feels like proximity reading, but sensations often appear faster and intuitive info arrives in blocks.

6. Systemic Energetic Reading (Global Reading)

Reading the entire **Body – Mind – Energy** system.

1. **Grounding**: Neutrality and breath.
2. **External Field (20–40 cm)**: Charges, mental agitation, relational tensions.
3. **Internal Field (0–5 cm)**: Memories, emotions, organic fatigue, densities.
4. **Nervous System**: Observe the rhythm (Too fast > stress; Too slow > deep fatigue).
5. **Breath**: The best indicator—where it doesn't flow, energy doesn't flow.

7. Full Tissue Reading (Protocol)

The "professional" version of tissue reading to read the body like an open book.

- **Step 1 – Global Scan**: Hands 10–15 cm above the body, head to toe. Locate "snagging" zones.

- **Step 2 – Entering the Tissue**: Descend to 2–3 cm. Perceive fine variations (tingling, dead zones, hyperactive zones).
- **Step 3 – Vertical Reading**:
    - Surface: Daily fatigue, recent stress.
    - Intermediate: Old emotions, accumulated tensions.
    - Core: Deep memories, blockages, old wounds.
- **Step 4 – Decoding**: Identify nature (emotional, mental, energetic, physical, ancestral, etc.).
- **Step 5 – Amplitude Evaluation**: Observe the "vibrational breath" (Wide = good; Reduced = tension; Absent = deep blockage).

8. The 12 Types of Vibrational Fields

An advanced diagnostic tool to understand which layer actually drives the person's state.

1. **Physical Field**: Dense. Sign: Body speaks (pains). Call: Grounding.
2. **Emotional Field**: Sign: Rapid reactions. Call: Regulation + Amplitude.
3. **Mental Field**: Sign: Thoughts dominate breath. Call: Slowing down + Clarity.
4. **Energetic Field**: Flows. Sign: Pulsations/Chills. Call: Fluidity.
5. **Vital Field**: Presence/Drive. Sign: Lack of motivation. Call: Reactivation.
6. **Soul Field**: Inner direction. Sign: Spontaneous intuition. Call: Heart/Crown axis.
7. **Spiritual Field**: Connection. Sign: Inspired thoughts. Call: High breathing.
8. **Informational Field**: Data/Memories. Sign: Repetitive patterns. Call: Update/Clearing.
9. **Relational Field**: Interaction. Sign: Sensitivity to vibes. Call: Coherence.
10. **Environmental Field**: Place. Sign: Fatigue in certain rooms. Call: Stabilization.
11. **Frequential Field**: Dominant "note." Sign: Being on a specific wavelength. Call: Tuning.
12. **Consciousness Field:** Perspective. Sign: Deep understanding. Call: Expansion.

9. HOW TO READ THE DIAGNOSIS?

Observe 3 things:

1. Which field speaks the l**oudest** (the most visible/agitated)?
2. Which field **actually drives** the current state (e.g., emotional anxiety driven by the Informational Field)?
3. Which field must be treated **first**? (Always the one that disorganizes the others).

10. Practitioner Version: Guided Consultation Protocol

- **Preparation**: Practitioner (Centering, "I read what is ready to be seen") / Consultant (Consent, Comfort).

- **Modes**: Use perceptive, intuitive, and semi-visual vision.
- **The Reading**: Manual scan, Express test, Detection of charged vs. weakened zones, Global system reading, and Full Tissue Reading.
- **Note**: Keep notes on zones to clear, rebalance, or reinforce. Reading is a map, not a judgment.

11. Self-Care: Energetic Reading & Self-Diagnosis (20–30 min)

- **Preparation:** Grounding and setting the intention of neutrality.
- **Scan**: External field scan, internal manual scan, observing the breath.
- **Depth**: Mental/Emotional observation followed by fine tissue reading (Surface > Intermediate > Deep).
- **Closing**: Expansion of your field like a mist of light, followed by gratitude to the body.

12. Practitioner + Hebrew Pendulum Protocol

Integrating dowsing for precise mapping.

- **Global Scan**: Manual scan confirmed by pendulum movement (Wide circle = balanced; Saccadic = tension; Weak = depleted).
- **Fine Decoding**: Passing the pendulum over each tissue layer to note amplitude and fluid irregularities.
- **Synthesis**: Note critical zones (emotional overload vs. physical blockage) to prepare the specific vibrational care protocol.

Self-Diagnosis with Hebrew Pendulum

A 20–30 minute protocol to read your own field. Use manual scanning first to "feel," then use the pendulum to "validate." Create a personal chart (Zone / Pendulum movement / Physical sensation / Priority) to guide your subsequent clearing or rebalancing.

PRACTICAL ADVICE: Never force the pendulum. Let the movement manifest naturally through your neutral presence.

CONCLUSION OF CHAPTER 5: You are now equipped to map the invisible. Whether on yourself or a client, you can identify the origin of a blockage rather than just its symptom. In the next chapter, we will learn the Transmutation Techniques to shift these identified frequencies.

CHAPTER 6
INTUITIVE BODY READING

|A| Part 1 : THE SENSOR AWAKENING

This text marks the transition from internal preparation to sensory action, transforming your own physiology into a high-precision diagnostic tool.

In previous chapters, we learned to stabilize our axis. Now, we are going to "turn on" the sensors. Vibrational Transition is based on one major premise: **your body knows everything.** It captures information long before your mind can put a word to it. Learning to read your body is learning to read the vibrational field of the living.

1. The Body as the "Ultimate Friend"

We have often been educated to perceive our body as a machine that needs fixing or, worse, as an obstacle that causes suffering. In Vibrational Transition, we radically change our perspective: the body is your Ultimate Friend, your most faithful ally.

- **Somatic Intelligence**: The body never lies. While the mind can tell itself stories or deny reality, your cells react instantaneously to a frequency.
- **The Radar-Body**: Consider your skin, your fascia, and your nervous system as a satellite dish. The body is the interface between the invisible world of frequencies and the visible world of matter.
- **The Toolless Approach**: By making your body your sole instrument, you eliminate filters. You no longer need to interpret the movement of a pendulum; you become the movement.

2. Decoding Vibrational Signals: The Alphabet of Feeling

To read the body, one must learn its language. Vibrational information translates into specific physical sensations:

- **Heat (Activation)**: The energy is flowing; it is "working." This often indicates a zone undergoing rebalancing or high vitality.
- **Density / Pressure (Blockage or Presence)**: The air feels thick, as if you are passing your hand through molasses or against a magnet. This indicates an accumulation of information or crystallized memory.
- **Emptiness / Cold (Lack)**: An air pocket, an absence of response, or a sudden chill. This signifies an energy leak or a disconnection in that specific area.
- **Tingling / "Pins and Needles" (Circulation)**: An electrical fizzing or "champagne bubbles." The signal is clear; information is passing through.

3. Self-Assessment: Measuring Your Vibration Without a Pendulum

How can you know if your Unity of Life (UL) is high or low without an external instrument? Use the **Sensory Echo** method.

- **Protocol**: Recenter yourself. Place your palms facing each other (10 cm apart). Slowly move them back and forth.

- **Analysis:** If your vibration is high, you will feel immediate resistance or an elastic ball of energy. If it is low, you will feel "nothing," as if your hands are moving through a vacuum.
- **Body Scan**: Close your eyes and ask: "What is my vibrational weather?" Observe which zone responds first—heavy shoulders or a light, open plexus?

|B| Part 2: EXPLORING THE BODY-INSTRUMENT

Now that your instrument is tuned, you can begin to perceive the vibrational reality of others. Intuitive body reading is not an intellectual analysis; it is **frequential listening**.

4. The Body as a Resonance Instrument

The practitioner does not "look at" the consultant; they enter into resonance with them.

- **The Biological Mirror**: Through mirror neurons and field entanglement, your body will "simulate" the consultant's frequencies. If they have tension in the plexus, you may feel a slight oppression in your own.
- **Signal vs. Noise**: The key is distinguishing your own background noise from the signals induced by the consultant. This is why the **Zero Point** is indispensable.

5. Perception Channels (Vibrational VAKOG)

- **Clair-sensation (Kinesthetic)**: Feeling variations in temperature, pressure, or density in your hands/body.
- **Clair-vision (Visual)**: Perceiving shadows, colors, or distortions in the aura (often as a mental image).
- **Clair-knowing** (Direct Intuition): Simply "knowing" instantly where the issue lies. A flash of thought: "It's the liver" or "It's unspoken sadness."

6. Methodology of the Vibrational Scan

1. **Calibration**: Stabilize your axis and ensure your UL is high. Set an intention of "Benevolent Neutrality."
2. **Distance Scan (Field Reading)**: Pass your hands 15-20 cm above the body. Look for "voids" (leaks) or "densities" (blockages).
3. **Tissue Scan (Matter Reading)**: With permission, place hands lightly on suspect zones. Listen to the rhythm. Healthy tissue "breathes" (expansion/retraction), while suffering tissue feels "frozen" or "electric."

7. Decoding Densities: The Language of Sensations

Sensation Perceived	**State of Information**	**Practitioner's Translation**
Tingling / Electricity	Info Overload	Vivid emotion, unexpressed anger, or recent inflammation. Energy is "pushing" to get out.
Density / Resistance	Crystallized Info	An old memory, rigid thought pattern, or past physical shock. The ultimate vibrational knot.

Sensation Perceived	State of Information	Practitioner's Translation
Cold / Emptiness	Absent Info	A zone of leakage or denial. The consultant has "withdrawn" consciousness from this part.
Gentle Heat / Vibration	Fluid Info	The zone is healthy and self-repairing. The flow circulates freely.

8. TRAINING EXERCISE: The "Blind" Reading

- **Goal**: Validate your feeling without visual or verbal cues.
- **Action**: Have a partner lie down. Close your eyes and scan 10 cm above them. Stop where your hand seems to "stop" on its own (magnet or hole sensation).
- **Validation**: Ask your partner: "What do you feel here right now?" or "Did something happen in this area recently?" You will often find your hand drawn to a forgotten scar or a silent pain.

SUMMARY FOR YOUR PRACTICE JOURNAL

- **Reading is not a Medical Diagnosis**: We observe states of fluidity or stagnation, not medical labels.
- **The Body is Global**: A blockage in the knee may originate in the pelvis or the emotional field.
- **Neutrality is Key**: If you care too much about being "right," you blur the signal. If you remain at Zero Point, the information comes to you.

Transition Note: Reading identified "WHERE" the issue is. In Chapter 7, we will learn to move the needle: using Conscious Intention to start moving these energies.

CHAPTER 7: THE MIND AS A MODULATOR

This text explores the interface between consciousness and matter, transforming mental intention into a concrete vibrational strike force.

If your body is the instrument (Chapter 4), your mind is the musician. In this chapter, we will discover that thought is not just an internal process, but a direct command sent to the vibrational field. Learning Vibrational Transition means learning to move from "**thought that undergoes**" to **"intention that modulates**."

|A| FROM "THOUGHT THAT UNDERGOES" TO "INTENTION THAT MODULATES"

1. Conscious Intention: The Rudder of Frequency

Intention is not a simple wish or desire. It is a precise vector direction. In energetics, it is often said that "energy follows attention." In Vibrational Transition, we refine this: "**energy takes the form of intention.**"

- **The Rudder**: Imagine a ship (your body) on an ocean of energy. Without conscious intention, you drift with the currents (others' emotions, collective stress). Intention is the rudder that imposes a direction.
- **Signal Clarity**: A fuzzy intention produces a fuzzy result. To modulate a frequency, the mind must be able to maintain a target image or sensation without wavering. This is called **non-dual focus**.

In training mode: Intention is not located in the forehead (mind) but must descend into the heart. A "mental" intention is weak; an "embodied" intention is irresistible.

2. The Role of Information in the Structure of Energy

Here lies the secret of the toolless method. Energy itself is "neutral," like modeling clay. What gives it shape, hardness, or fluidity is Information.

- **Energy is the carrier, information is the message**: Just as electricity carries sound through a phone wire, your vital energy carries informational codes.
- **Informational "Cysts"**: Chronic pain is often energy carrying obsolete information (a past fear, a shock).
- **Deprogramming**: To change a physical state, the practitioner must not only "send energy," they must re-inform the zone. By changing the information (through the intention of peace, fluidity, or liberation), the vibrational structure changes, and matter follows.

3. Moving from Thought to Pure Vibration

The beginner's greatest challenge is to extract themselves from "verbal thought" (talking to oneself in the head) to enter "**pure vibration**."

- **Verbal Thought (Level 1)**: You say to yourself: "I want this pain to go away." This is a mental order, often tinged with resistance, which creates little effect because it stays on the surface.
- **Imagery (Level 2)**: You visualize the area lighting up. This is more powerful because the brain treats images as biological realities.
- **Pure Vibration (Level 3 - The Goal)**: You no longer think, you no longer visualize: **you resonate**. You become the frequency of healing yourself. If you want to bring fluidity to an organ, you contact the sensation of fluidity within yourself (like flowing water) and let that sensation radiate from your hands or your presence.

4. The Transition Triad: Attention, Intention, Direction

For the mind to become an effective modulator, it must learn to synchronize three distinct functions:

- **Attention (The Diagnosis)**: The ability to maintain focused consciousness on a specific area without the mind wandering. If your attention escapes, the "bridge" between you and the consultant breaks.
- **Intention (The Quality)**: The information you inject into the channel. It defines what to do (e.g., "Dissolve," "Calm," "Reactivate").
- **Direction (The Vector)**: The movement you impose on the energy. Energy must not only be present; it must know where to go (toward the earth, toward another organ, or toward the expansion of the field).

5. The Mechanism of "Frequential Command"

In training, we learn that the practitioner is not a healer, but a **reference transmitter.**

1. **Command through the Void**: Instead of imagining you are sending something (which exhausts your own reserves), you create a vibrational "vacuum." By reaching the **Zero Point** in your mind, you create a zone of silence so perfect that the consultant's blockage naturally draws in this peace to balance itself.
2. **Using the Inner Verb**: The "Verb" is structured vibration. By using mental keywords during modulation, you give a geometric shape to your intention.
    - "Release": For an emotion that clings.
    - "Open": For physical congestion or a tissue knot.
    - "Source": For a devitalized zone, calling upon the telluric current.

6. Informational Transition

At this stage of practice, we transition from physical action to informational influence. We no longer act *upon* the body, but rather communicate with the consciousness that governs it. This is the moment where the mind begins to propose new frequency options to the biological system.

7. MODULATION EXERCISE: The Laser and the Diffusion

Objective: To master mental focus in order to act on areas of different sizes.

- **The Laser**: Choose a very small area (a scar, a finger joint). Concentrate your entire intention on this single point, as if you wanted to pass a very fine thread of light through it. Feel the density of the response.
- **The Diffusion**: Suddenly broaden your intention to the partner's entire body. Feel how the energy changes texture: it becomes less "sharp" but more enveloping.
- **The Alternation**: Switch between the two three times. A good practitioner must know how to alternate between **surgical precision and global harmonization.**

8. PRACTITIONER PRECAUTION: The Neutrality of Intention

The fatal error would be to inject personal will into the intention.

- If you say to yourself: "I absolutely want him to stop hurting," you are no longer a modulator; you are a **savior.**
- The "**Savior**" uses their own Life Unit, which leads to burnout.
- The "**Modulator**" remains neutral. They present the frequency of health and leave the client free to embrace it or not.

9. TRAINING EXERCISE: Palm Modulation

Objective: To physically verify the impact of the mind on energy.

1. Place your left hand in front of you, palm facing up.
2. **Phase 1 ("Heaviness" Information)**: Think intensely of a lead weight, of dark density. Feel your hand become heavy and compact. Note the signals (slow tingling, dull heat).
3. **Phase 2 ("Lightness" Information)**: Change instantly. Think of a feather, of pure air, of a helium bubble. Feel your hand become airy, almost non-existent.

Observation: Your muscles did not move, but your physical sensation changed radically. This is modulation.

Harmonization Note: This chapter lays the mental foundation for everything that follows. Without mastery of the modulating mind, manual techniques are merely gymnastics.

|B| INTENTION AND CELLULAR MEMORY

10. Rewriting the Code of Matter

A pain is merely an error message in the body's operating system. Modulating with the mind is like correcting a line of computer code. If the body believes it must remain in a state of "contraction" following a past shock, your mind presents a new option: "**fluidity**." Through resonance, the consultant's body recognizes this option as its true nature and adopts it instantly. This is the **Sovereignty of the Mind over Frequency.**

11. The Three Levels of Resonance

To move into **Pure Vibration (Level 3)**, your simple presence in the room must "inform" the field. The transition occurs through **frequential entrainment**: the more ordered state (yours) entrains the disordered state (the blockage) to align itself.

12. TRAINING PROTOCOL: Transmutation of the Verb

- **Enunciation**: Choose a keyword (e.g., Fluidity).
- **Sensation**: Feel where this word "resonates" in your body. Feel the texture of fluidity.
- **Expansion:** Drop the word. Keep only the sensation.
- **Projection**: Direct this pure sensation toward a zone of density.

13. Cellular Memory: Deprogramming the Invisible

When a traumatic event occurs, if the emotion is not evacuated, the "danger" information freezes. The cell continues to vibrate as if the shock were still present. Conscious intention acts here as an "eraser" or a "re-writer."

14. The De-crystallization Process

1. **Recognition (Witnessing)**: Your intention sees the memory. "I feel this memory, I recognize your signal." This alone reduces the charge by 50%.
2. **Dissolution through Presence**: Envelop the memory. Do not tear it away; dilute it. Key intention: "You can let go now, the event is over."
3. **Re-information (Health Imprint)**: Project Fluidity or Peace into the newly emptied space.

15. PRACTICAL EXERCISE: The Silent Cellular Dialogue

- **Locate**: Identify a chronic tension (stomach, throat, etc.).
- **Contact**: Place your hand and sink your consciousness inside the skin.
- **Inquiry**: Mentally ask the area: "What frequency are you carrying?"
- **Modulation**: Breathe into the zone. On each exhale, send an intention of "Update." Say internally: "Update to the present."
- **Observe**: Feel the moment the tissue "gives" (a sensation of heat or a deep sigh).

SUMMARY OF CHAPTER 7

The modulating mind is the tool of Sovereignty. The practitioner who masters their mind no longer "works"; they **emit**. They become a living tuning fork. By adjusting their own frequency through conscious intention, they offer the world a reference of coherence.

Transition Note: Your mind is now capable of modulating the invisible. In the next section, we will apply these principles to the specific techniques of energy movement.

PART III: RELEASE AND PURIFICATION

CHAPTER 8
CLEANING - RELEASE AND NEUTRALIZATION

This chapter constitutes the operational core of the "cleansing" phase. It transforms frequency concepts into concrete actions for purifying the cellular and etheric structure.

After learning to listen **(Body Reading)** and to direct **(The Modulating Mind)**, the practitioner enters the active phase of the Transition: the purification of the terrain. In this chapter, we no longer approach the body as a solid mass, but as an information storage system that needs to be updated.

1. Vibrational Neutralization of Toxins and Memories

Before addressing deep-seated pathologies or ancient "Crystallized Memories," the practitioner must first clear the consultant's "vibrational dust." This process—known as **Sweeping**—prepares the terrain by removing the informational noise of daily life.

1. UNDERSTANDING VIBRATIONAL TOXINS

Everything we experience leaves a trace. In the "Profession of Living," we distinguish between two types of burdens that lower an individual's **Life Unit (LU)**:

- **Surface Toxins (Gas Toxins):** These are volatile residues—work stress, electromagnetic pollution, or emotional "smog" encountered in the street. They float in the periphery of the field (the aura) and saturate the lungs and plexus. They are often evacuated through yawning or deep breathing.
- **Crystallized Memories (Crystal Toxins):** These are "ancient" toxins lodged in the fascia, joints, and deep organs (liver, kidneys). They consist of information from shocks, grief, or fears that were never processed. They act as "clots" in the circulation of energy.

2. THE PRINCIPLE: NEUTRALIZATION (NOT FIGHTING)

To neutralize is not to "fight." In **Vibrational Transition**, we use the **Law of Frequency Opposition**.

- **The Mechanism:** If an area is saturated by a jagged frequency (e.g., Anger), the practitioner responds with a coherent, stable frequency (Deep Peace).
- **The Result:** Through resonance, your coherent frequency absorbs and neutralizes the dissonant one. This is the **Reset to Zero**. You are like water flowing over a dirty stone: the water remains water; it does not become the mud—it simply carries it toward the earth to be recycled.

3. THE OPERATIONAL PROTOCOL: THE SWEEPING GESTURE

Objective: To clear the space so that life can express itself again. One cannot re-inform a field that is saturated with "noise."

- **The Action:** Use **Transverse Passes**. Your hands act like rakes or combs moving through the subtle layers of the aura.
- **The Gesture:** 1. Start from the central axis of the body.

  2. Spread your hands sharply and firmly outward toward the periphery of the consultant's field.

  3. Imagine you are tearing through a heavy veil of mist or clearing a crowded workbench.
- **The Intention (The Word):** *"I clear this space. Everything that does not belong to this Life Unit is evacuated and returned to the Source."*
- **The Sign of Success:** You will perceive a change in luminosity or a sudden sensation of lightness. The field, previously "sticky" or dense, becomes fluid and transparent.

4. BEYOND THE SURFACE: THE DISSOLUTION POINT

For toxins that have descended into the tissues (fascia, muscles, organs), sweeping is the prerequisite for **Targeted Neutralization**:

1. **Identification:** Place two fingers on an area felt as "dense" or "cold."
2. **Immobilization:** Remain perfectly still. Do not try to "move" the energy.
3. **Absorption (Vibrational Osmosis):** Visualize your hand as blotting paper. It attracts the information toward the **Zero Point**, where it is instantly disintegrated.
4. **Release:** The process is complete when you feel a "pulsation" under your fingers, signaling that the tissue has regained its natural frequency.

SUMMARY FOR YOUR PRACTICE JOURNAL

Phase	Action	Vibrational Purpose
Neutralizing	Bringing to Zero	Establishing coherence over dissonance.
Sweeping	Transverse Passes	Removing surface "Gas Toxins" and daily stress.
Purifying	Fixed Imposition	Dissolving deep "Crystal Toxins" in organs/bones.

PRACTITIONER'S ADVICE:

Cleansing is an act of **Neutral Compassion**. If you cleanse with disgust or fear of being "soiled," you lower your own frequency and become vulnerable. Stay centered in your axis; you are a translucent canal, not a sponge.

Transition Note: Once the terrain is cleansed and the "dust" is removed, the practitioner can move to the next step: **The Release of Flows**, ensuring energy circulates where it was previously cut off.

2. Detoxification of Tissues and Subtle Organs

1. Cleansing:

Must occur on several levels simultaneously to be definitive.

- **The Tissue Level (Physical)**: Fascia and muscles store lactic acid and emotional toxins. Vibrational detoxification consists of making the tissues "vibrate" through intention to restart lymphatic and energetic circulation.
- **The Subtle Organ Level**: Each organ has its own frequency signature. The liver manages anger and filtering; the lungs manage sadness and exchange. When we "detox" an organ, we cleanse both its biological load and its associated emotional load.
- **Vibrational Blood**: Blood is the primary vector of information in the body. Cleansing the blood field allows the new health information to be diffused throughout the organism in just a few minutes.

While surface cleansing resembles sweeping, **tissue detoxification** is akin to vibrational osmosis. Here, the practitioner helps the physical body expel what it has accumulated at the cellular level.

2. "Crystal Toxins" vs. "Gas Toxins"

- Gas Toxin (Emotional): Volatile. It saturates the lungs and the plexus. It is evacuated through breath and yawning.
- Crystal Toxin (Physical/Memory): Lodged in the fascia, joints, and deep organs (liver, kidneys). It requires a slower and more insistent frequency to be "dislodged."

3. Cleansing the Subtle Organs

Every physical organ possesses a vibrational "double." The liver stores undigested anger, the kidneys store ancestral fears, and the lungs store sadness.

In Training Mode: Detoxing an organ does not consist of acting on its chemistry, but of "cleaning its filter." An organ saturated with negative information can no longer fulfill its biological function optimally because its command signal is scrambled.

4. TECHNICAL PROTOCOL: Detoxification by Resonance Vibration

Objective: To dislodge informational impurities from the heart of matter.

- **The Receptive Hand and the Emitting Hand**:
    - Place your left hand (**receptive**) under the consultant's back, level with the target organ (e.g., the liver).
    - Place your right hand (**emitting**) above the organ, on the abdomen.
- **Creating the Current**:
    - Imagine a flow of pure energy crossing the organ between your two hands.
- **Setting the Vibration**:
    - Apply a very slight physical vibration with your right hand while emitting an intention of "**Dissolution of dross**."
    - The movement must be so fine that it resembles a cellular shimmering.
- **Evacuation**:

- Once you feel the area becoming "softer" or "more fluid," use your intention to direct these toxins toward the body's natural emunctories (liver, kidneys, skin) or directly toward the earth.

5. Releasing "Shock Memories" in the Tissues

- Tissues keep traces of impacts (accidents, surgeries). Even if the scar is closed, the tissue still vibrates at the "**impact frequency**."
- **The Inhibition Point Technique**: Maintain very light pressure on the area of the scar or the old pain.
- **The Effect**: By maintaining a frequency of **Safety and Neutrality**, you inform the tissue that "the alert is over." The cell stops contracting, and metabolic toxins accumulated by chronic contraction are finally released into the circulation to be eliminated.

PRACTICE ADVICE: Managing "Healing Crises"

Be aware that effective detoxification can lead to an immediate reaction from the consultant.

- **Physical signs**: Coughing, sudden heat, borborygmi (intestinal gurgling), or even a liberating tear.
- **Practitioner Attitude**: Do not stop the process. Welcome these signs as proof that the Transition is underway. Encourage the consultant to exhale deeply to support the evacuation of toxins.

SUMMARY FOR PRACTICE JOURNAL

- **The Organ is an antenna**: if it is dirty, it poorly receives the Life Unit.
- **Fine Vibration** is the key to dislodging tissue densities.
- **Evacuation** must always be directed (downward or toward an exit).

Transition Note: The terrain is now clean and the organs are discharged. We can move to the heart of the transformation.

3. Active Phase of Purification

The practitioner learns to distinguish "material" toxins from "informational" toxins.

Once the diagnosis is made and the intention is sealed, the first concrete act of care is **Cleansing**. One cannot re-inform a field that is saturated with "noise" or residue. To cleanse is to clear the space so that life can express itself once again.

1. Vibrational Neutralization of Toxins and Memories

It is crucial to understand that everything surrounding us leaves a trace. We are not only the result of what we eat, but also of what we vibrate and receive.

2. The Nature of "Vibrational Toxins"

There are two types of burdens that lower an individual's Life Unit (LU):

- **Surface Toxins**: These are the residues of daily life—work stress, electromagnetic pollution, or negative thoughts encountered in the street. They float in the periphery of the field (the aura).

- **Crystallized Memories**: These are "ancient" toxins. They have descended into the depths of the tissues. They consist of information from shocks, grief, or fears that were never evacuated. They act as "clots" in the circulation of energy.

3. The Principle of Neutralization

Neutralizing does not mean "fighting." In Vibrational Transition, we neutralize through the Law of Frequency Opposition.

- If an area is saturated by a memory of "Anger" (a fast and jagged frequency), the practitioner does not respond with force.
- Instead, they generate a frequency of "**Deep Peace**" (a slow and stable frequency).
- When the two frequencies meet, the most coherent one (yours) absorbs and neutralizes the most dissonant one. This is the principle of resetting to zero.

4. Neutralizing Deep Memories: The Dissolution Point

For memories anchored in organs or bones, sweeping is not enough. Targeted Neutralization must be performed.

- **Identification**: Place two fingers on the area identified as "dense" or "cold."
- **Immobilization**: Remain perfectly still. Do not try to move the energy.
- **Absorption**: Visualize your hand as a blotting paper. It does not suck in the pain (to avoid polluting yourself); it attracts the information toward the Zero Point, where it is instantly disintegrated.
- **Release**: The neutralization is complete when you feel a "pulsation" under your fingers. This is the sign that the tissue has regained its own frequency of life.

ADVICE

Cleansing is not an act of power; it is an act of **Neutral Compassion**. If you cleanse with "preconceptions," you lower your own frequency and become vulnerable.

Cleanse as you would let water flow over a dirty stone: the water remains water; it does not become the mud—it simply carries it away toward the earth to be recycled.

SUMMARY FOR PRACTICE JOURNAL

- **Neutralizing** = Bringing back to zero frequency through coherence.
- **Releasing** = Removing surface layers (Transverse Passes).
- **Purifying** = Dissolving deep memories (Fixed Imposition).

Transition Note: Once the terrain is cleansed, we can move to the next step: **The Release of Flows**. In the remainder of Chapter 8, we will see how to restart circulation where it has been cut off.

CONCLUSION OF CHAPTER 8

OPERATIONAL SYNTHESIS: THE CLEANING DYNAMIC

The act of cleaning is not merely a preliminary step; it is a full therapeutic act. By removing the "vibrational noise" and the "informational clots" (toxins and memories), you allow the consultant's **Life Unit (LU)** to regain its natural resonance. As a practitioner, your mastery of this chapter lies in your ability to distinguish between surface residues and deep crystallizations.

Key Takeaways for Your Practice:

1. **Vacuum vs. Substance:** You do not "remove" an illness; you neutralize the frequency that supports it. By establishing a **Zero Point** in a dense area, you create a vibrational vacuum where the memory can no longer exist.
2. **The Priority of Flow:** Always start with the **Surface Cleansing (Sweeping)**. It is futile to attempt deep cellular work if the aura is saturated with the "static" of daily stress. Clear the fog before you try to heal the organ.
3. **Neutral Compassion:** Your effectiveness is dictated by your posture. If you judge the toxin, you attach yourself to it. If you observe it with neutrality, it dissolves.

PRACTITIONER'S CHECKLIST

- **Step 1 (Neutralization):** Did I reach the Zero Point before starting?
- **Step 2 (Sweeping):** Have I performed the Transverse Passes to clear the peripheral field?
- **Step 3 (Dissolution):** Have I identified and "melted" the deep points of cold or density?
- **Step 4 (Validation):** Do I feel the "tissue breath" or the return of pulsation in the treated area?

TRANSITION TO THE NEXT STAGE:

Cleaning is the act of **clearing the path**. Now that the obstacles have been neutralized, the energy must be put back into motion. In the following section, we will study the **Release of Flows**, moving from the "Static" of purification to the "Dynamic" of vital circulation.

"The space is now free. Let life flow where it was once frozen."

CHAPTER 9
TISSUE AND INFORMATIONAL READING

- **Understanding information stored in matter** (bones, muscles, organs).
- **Clearing crystallized emotional charges.**
- **The 3 Elements Exercise** (Earth, Water, Air) for fluidity.

This chapter bridges the gap between physical sensation (matter) and invisible data (information), transforming the practitioner into a true "reader" of the living.

After cleaning the global field with the sweep (Chapter 8), we now enter the surgical precision of **Vibrational Transition**. Tissue reading is the art of listening to what the body has "recorded" beyond words. This is where the toolless approach takes on its full dimension: your hands become interfaces capable of decoding the memories of matter.

1. Understanding Information Stored in Matter

The body is not just flesh and bone; it is a **biological library**. Every significant event and unresolved stress leaves an informational footprint in the physical structure. Think of the body as a **living crystal**. Matter is not inert; it is a condensation of energy that possesses memory.

1. Bone: Structural and Ancestral Memory

Bone is the densest part of our incarnation. Vibrationally, it carries the oldest information:

- **Family patterns**: What we carry "in our genes" or "in our bones."
- **Deep shocks**: Traumas that have shaken our foundations.
- **Practitioner's feel**: Under the hand, a bone saturated with heavy information feels "cold," "immobile," or "leaden." A healthy bone vibrates with a dull but powerful frequency.

2. Muscle: Emotional and Reactive Memory

The muscle is the seat of action and protection. It stores "fight or flight" memories:

- **Accumulated stress**: Retained anger often lodges in the back and jaw muscles.
- **Armoring**: Muscles harden to protect a vulnerable emotion.
- **Practitioner's feel**: A muscle "informed" by fear will be hard, fibrous, or exhibit an electrical twitch (fasciculation) as soon as it is approached.

3. The Organ: Biographical and Alchemical Memory

Beyond simple emotion, organs store life scenarios:

- **Liver**: Feelings of injustice and chronic anger.
- **Stomach**: Situations that one cannot "digest."
- **Lungs**: Territory and the ability to take one's place.
- **Practitioner's feel**: A saturated organ gives a "doughy" or "foggy" sensation during vibrational palpation.

2. Clearing Crystallized Emotional Charges

An emotional charge is energy that was unable to complete its movement cycle. It has "**crystallized**," becoming a zone of low frequency and high density. Imagine an unexpressed emotion acting like a drop of resin that hardens over time, imprisoning muscle fibers or cells.

1. The Mechanism of Crystallization

When a shock occurs, if the energy is not evacuated through movement, screaming, or crying, it "freezes."

- **Physical**: The fascia retracts, and blood circulation decreases.
- **Vibrational:** The frequency of the area drops and loops (the "scratched record" effect). The body spends constant energy maintaining this "knot," causing the global **Unity of Life** to drop.

2. Technique: The Liberation Point Protocol

We use **Harmonic Resonance** to melt the crystallization through a coherent frequency.

1. **The Entry Point**: Place two fingers (index and middle) on the densest point of the crystallization.
2. **Phasing**: Breathe with the area. On the inhale, connect to the tension. On the exhale, send a wave of Neutral Presence.
3. **The Call for Movement**: Imagine the charge vibrating faster and faster. You don't force the movement; you allow it.
4. **The Release**: Manifests as a muscle twitch, a wave of heat, or a deep involuntary sigh. The "resin" has melted.

3. Storage Mapping (Where to look):

- **Solar Plexus**: Frustrations and powerlessness.
- **Pelvis**: "The muscle of the soul"—visceral fears and survival/intimacy trauma.
- **Shoulders/Trapezius**: The weight of responsibility and retained anger.
- **Throat**: Unspoken words and hindered self-expression.

3. TECHNIQUE: The 3 Elements Exercise (Earth, Water, Air)

Once memories are dislodged, tissues may remain in a state of "stun" or emptiness. To prevent the body from recreating its old armor, use the vibrational analogy of the 3 Elements to re-inform the matter.

Element	Focus	Application & Frequency
1. EARTH	Structure	**Stabilize**. Firm but gentle pressure. Restores security and "seals" the release into the flesh. Frequency: Low, stable, grounding.
2. WATER	Circulation	**Flow**. Micro-undulation or light pumping. Rinses residues of emotional dross through the lymph. Frequency: Fluid, rhythmic, cleansing.
3. AIR	Space	**Expand.** Hands rise a few centimeters above the skin.

Element	Focus	Application & Frequency
		Clears the "energetic fog" and relanches vitality. Frequency: High, subtle, expansive.

4. The "Dance of the Elements" Synthesis:

- **Immobilization (Earth)**: For 1 minute, stabilize. Feel the weight.
- **Undulation (Water)**: For 1 minute, restart movement. Feel the fluidity.
- **Expansion (Air)**: For 1 minute, lighten pressure. Feel the radiance.

Success Sign: The tissue is no longer just "soft"; it is **vibrant.**

SUMMARY FOR YOUR PRACTICE JOURNAL:

- **Bone** = Foundations (Ancestral).
- **Muscle** = Reactions (Emotional).
- **Organ** = Experiences (Biographical).
- **Earth** = I stabilize (Security).
- **Water** = I circulate (Cleaning).
- **Air** = I expand (Lightness).

PRACTITIONER ADVICE:

Tissue reading requires absolute neutrality. If you fear what you might find, or if you desperately want to "heal" at all costs, you create mental noise that blurs the information.

CONCLUSION OF CHAPTER 9

OPERATIONAL SYNTHESIS: FROM LISTENING TO UNDERSTANDING

Tissue and informational reading is the act of "becoming a witness" to the consultant's reality. This chapter has taught you that the body never lies; it is a living map where every tension, every cold zone, and every energetic void tells a story. Your role is not to interpret these signs intellectually, but to feel them in order to identify the root frequency of the imbalance.

Key Points to Remember for Your Practice:

1. **Listening Precedes Action:** Never begin a treatment before "reading" the terrain. An intervention without prior reading is a blind intervention that risks jolting the consultant's system rather than supporting it.
2. **Sensing is Not Imagination:** Whether through Clear-Sensing, thermal detection, or the perception of densities, trust your hands. If you feel "cold," there is a crystallization; if you feel "wind," there is a leak.
3. **The Right Distance:** Reading is done with respect for energetic privacy. Learn to navigate between the distal field (the aura) and physical contact to obtain a multidimensional view of the Unity of Life (UL).

PRACTICE JOURNAL: YOUR READING GRID

- **Heat Zone:** Inflammation, anger, energy surplus (needs dispersion).

- **Cold Zone:** Ancient memory, crystallized shock, vitality void (needs re-information).
- **"Mass" Zone:** Vibrational toxicity, dense physical or emotional blockage.
- **"Void" Zone:** Energetic leak, disconnection from the body, loss of sovereignty.

TRANSITION TO ACTION:

Now that you know how to "read" the body and decode its messages, you are ready to act with precision. The reading has revealed the obstacles; the next chapter, Chapter 10 – Magnetic Passes and Flow Direction, will provide you with the tools to put life back into motion and restore circulation where it had stopped.

"To read the body is to listen to the soul's song through matter. Once the song is heard, harmony can be restored."

PART IV: TRANSMISSION TECHNIQUES (THE CRAFT)

CHAPTER 10: MAGNETIC PASSES

This chapter is crucial as it integrates magnetic passes as a rebalancing tool while maintaining the spirit of "Vibrational Transition," where intention and feeling take precedence over mechanical gestures.

In this chapter, we address the technical dimension of the "Transitor" craft. While Vibrational Transition occurs primarily through the mind and presence, the movement of the hands within the energy field—known as magnetic passes—allows for the structuring, directing, and stabilizing of flow in a way that is both visible and tactile for the consultant's body.

A. REBALANCING TECHNIQUES: The Gestures of Flow

Magnetic passes are movements performed with the hands at a distance ranging from a few centimeters to thirty centimeters from the physical body. They act as informational vectors that "comb" or "order" vibrational currents.

1. Longitudinal Passes (Soothing and Diffusion)

The fundamental movement to calm and distribute energy evenly.

- **The Gesture**: Hands start at the crown of the head and descend slowly, fluidly, and continuously to the feet (or fingertips if the person is lying down).
- **The Vibrational Effect**: They act like a "serenity shower," smoothing out rough spots in the etheric field and diffusing energy where it is lacking.
- **Training Mode**: Use these at the end of a session to seal the work, or at the beginning to calm an overactive nervous system (stress, anxiety). Speed must be constant and slow.

2. Transverse Passes (Breaking Blockages)

A dynamic technical gesture used to break up stagnation and release zones of intense congestion. Unlike longitudinal passes, these are sharp and perpendicular to the body's axis.

- **The Gesture**: A "shearing" or rapid sweeping movement from the inside toward the outside (like drawing curtains or brushing away dust).
- **The Vibrational Effect**: Used to "break" overly dense energy accumulations. If a pain is localized and feels "stagnant," the transverse pass shatters the informational crystallization.
- **Training Mode**: Never perform transverse passes on an "empty" or exhausted zone. Use them only where you have detected "density" or "stagnant heat" during your tissue reading.

3. The Nature of the Gesture: "Tearing the Veil"

The transverse pass acts as a vibrational scalpel. While longitudinal passes glide over blockages, the "shearing" movement is required to break resistance.

- **Rupture Effect:** Breaks surface crystallizations and heat accumulations (inflammations).

- **Disconnection Effect:** Ideal for freeing a consultant from an obsessive thought or a burdensome relational cord "hooked" to their field.
- **Awakening Effect:** Shakes up dormant energies; used to "wake up" a numb limb or an atonic zone.

4. Technical Protocol: The Release Gesture

1. **Focus on the Knot:** Identify the congestion (plexus, forehead, throat). Bring joined hands to 10 cm from the area, palms facing the body.
2. **Vivid Expansion:** Separate hands with a sharp snap to the right and left. Accompany this with a brief, audible exhale through the mouth.
3. **Debris Evacuation:** At the end of the movement, flick your fingers toward the ground (away from the consultant) to project energetic residues to the earth.
4. **Frequency:** Repeat 3 to 5 times until the air between your hands feels "fluid" and less resistant.

5. When to Use the Transverse Pass?

- **On the Forehead:** To dissipate tension migraines or mental "traffic jams."
- **On the Plexus:** To release a "ball of anxiety" or a blocked emotion hindering breath.
- **On Acute Pain:** To disperse excess nerve charge (inflammation).
- **At Session's End:** To "cut" the link between practitioner and consultant.

B. PALM IMPOSITION VS. DISTANCE SWEEPING

In Vibrational Transition, the choice between **Imposition** (contact or immediate proximity) and **Sweeping** (distance movement) determines your impact. It is the difference between feeding an organ and cleaning a field.

1. Imposition: Frequential Nutrition

A fixed act of condensation. By staying still, you create a "bridge of coherence." Energy accumulates until the consultant's area reaches the same vibrational level as yours (homeostasis by resonance).

- **Palmar Imposition (The Palm)**: For large areas (stomach, back). Brings calm and heat.
- **Digital Imposition (The Fingers)**: For precise points (temples, vertebrae). Brings precision and penetration.
- **"V" Imposition**: Hands surround a joint or the head. Creates a closed regeneration circuit.

2. Distance Sweeping: Mastery of Space

An act of expansion. As you move further from the physical body (up to 1 meter), you influence subtler layers, psychic structures, and distant memories.

- **The "Breeze" Effect**: Distance sweeping moves stagnant energy. It is the ideal tool to "de-saturate" a consultant who feels oppressed or heavy.

3. Comparison Table: Which Technique to Choose?

Characteristic	Imposition (Fixed)	Sweeping (Movement)
Objective	Fill, warm, stabilize.	Clean, disperse, smooth.
Physical Effect	Pain relief, tissue repair.	Nervous relaxation, mental clarity.
Target	Organs, bones, local injuries.	Emotional field, global aura.
Sensation	Heat, soothing heaviness.	Coolness, light breeze, tingling.

4. Technical Protocol: The Imposition-Sweeping Transition

For maximum effectiveness, combine both:

1. **Initial Sweep**: Clean the area (prepare the terrain).
2. **Imposition**: Nourish the area (provide health information).
3. **Final Sweep**: Smooth and distribute surplus (harmonization).

5. PRACTITIONER'S ADVICE: The Neutrality of the Rupture

Do not confuse "speed" with "aggression." Your gesture must be vivid, but your internal state must remain at **Zero Point**. Effectiveness comes from the **speed of intention**, not the strength of the arm.

Summary for your Practice Journal:

- **Transverse Pass** = Action of rupture and dispersion.
- **Imposition** = A battery: it recharges the voids.
- **Sweeping** = Evacuates the clutter.
- **Movement** = From center to exterior, vivid and sharp.

Transition Note: You now know how to smooth (longitudinal) and release (transverse). Next, we will learn how to focus energy on a precise point to nourish the organs.

C. HARMONIZING ENERGETIC POLES

The human body is polarized (Top/Bottom, Right/Left, Front/Back). A successful Transition requires harmonizing these poles so that the **Unity of Life** circulates in a closed, efficient circuit.

- **North Pole / South Pole**: By placing one hand on the crown of the head and the other on the soles of the feet (or the sacrum), the practitioner creates a frequential "bridge." This restores the Vertical Axis discussed in Chapter 3.
- **The Emitting Hand and the Receiving Hand**: Generally, your dominant hand (right for right-handed people) "emits" the transition information, while the other "listens" to the body's reaction. Harmonizing the poles is sensing the moment the flow between your two hands becomes homogeneous, creating a positive feedback loop.

1. Vibrational Symmetry

The human body functions like a living magnet. It possesses polarity: a positive pole (often the top and right side) and a negative pole (the bottom and left side). Health depends on the free circulation between these poles. If energy accumulates at the top (headaches, stress) or stagnates at the bottom (heaviness, lack of drive), the system is in "polarity disharmony."

- **The Role of Harmonization**: The goal is no longer to clean or nourish, but to redistribute. It is the art of creating a closed circuit so that the Unity of Life (UV) self-balances through the principle of communicating vessels.

2. The "Bridge-Hands" Technique

This technique is generally practiced at the end of a session to stabilize all previous work.

- **Hand Polarity**: In traditional magnetism, the right hand is often considered the emitter (+) and the left hand the receiver (-).
- **Diagonal Positioning**:
  - Place one hand on the right shoulder and the other on the left hip.
  - Maintain the position for 2 to 3 minutes.
  - Reverse the position (left shoulder and right hip).
- **Intention**: To become a "jumper cable." You give nothing; you simply allow the consultant's current to flow from point A to point B through your own neutrality.

3. Sky-Earth Balancing (The Final Verticality)

Once the lateral poles are harmonized, the practitioner must seal the vertical axis. This prevents the consultant from feeling "floaty" when leaving the session.

- **The Anchor Point**: Place one hand on the crown (Crown Chakra) and the other at the base of the spine (Sacrum) or on the soles of the feet.
- **Visualizing the Flow:** Feel the energy descending like a waterfall from the summit to the base.
- **The End Signal**: You will know the poles are harmonized when you feel an identical pulsation in both hands. This is the Synchronization of Vibrational Pulses.

D. TRAINING PROTOCOL: The Rapid Rebalancing Session

Detailed complete transmission protocols (Contact, Mentalized, Emergency).

1. **Rupture Phase**: 3 rapid transverse passes over detected tension zones.
2. **Saturation Phase**: Palm imposition on the Solar Plexus (emotional center) for 2 minutes with an intention of "Peace."
3. **Smoothing Phase**: 5 slow longitudinal passes from head to toe to harmonize the whole.
4. **Polarization Phase**: One hand on the forehead, one hand on the stomach until equal heat is felt in both palms.

THE GESTURE AS A VECTOR

Passes are not "magic gestures"; they are supports for your intention. If your hands move but your mind is elsewhere, the effect will be zero. Conversely, a single pass made with total presence can unblock situations that have been settled for years.

1. Longitudinal Passes (Soothing and Diffusion)

The fundamental gesture of harmonization. It consists of a fluid, continuous movement that travels the body from top to bottom.

- **The Nature of the Gesture**: Imagine smoothing a wrinkled sheet. The hand must be supple, fingers slightly spread but relaxed, acting as precision sensors.
- **Soothing Effect**: Slow descent calms the nervous system. It helps the consultant "land" back in their body after intense emotional release. Ideal for insomnia and anxiety.
- **Diffusion Effect**: If a specific zone was treated (e.g., the liver), energy might be too concentrated there. The longitudinal pass takes this excess light and redistributes it harmoniously.

2. Technical Protocol: Mastering the Flow

- **Distance Calibration**:
  - 5-10 cm: Acts on the etheric body (physical vitality). Ideal for fatigue and physical pain.
  - 20-30 cm: Acts on the emotional body. Ideal for mental agitation and stress.
- **Speed of Gesture**:
  - **Slow**: Sedative. Slows down overactive energy (stress, hypertension).
  - **Fast**: Toning. Wakes up an atonic zone or a lethargic consultant.
- **The Flow Exit (Sealing)**: Every pass must imperatively end beyond the consultant's feet. Never stop abruptly in the middle of the body.

3. Two Variants of the Longitudinal Pass

- **The Large Current Pass**: Encompasses the whole body. Used at the start and end of a session to create a "vibrational cocoon."
- **The Segmental Pass**: Focuses on a specific part (e.g., shoulder to fingertips). Used to "drain" local pain toward the extremity to expel it from the field.

4. Practitioner Advice: Posture and Breath

- **Movement comes from the legs**: Do not just use your arms. Accompany the movement with your whole body, knees supple.
- **Synchronized Breath**: Inhale as you raise your hands to the head, and exhale long and slow throughout the downward gesture. Your breath is the motor that "pushes" the magnetism.

SUMMARY FOR YOUR PRACTICE JOURNAL

- **Longitudinal Passes**: Global smoothing and harmonization (Calm).
- **Transverse Passes**: Breaking and releasing (The Cut).
- **Impositions**: Nourishing and focusing (The Full).
- **Pole Harmonization**: Distributing and stabilizing (The Balance).

CONCLUSION OF CHAPTER 10

OPERATIONAL SYNTHESIS: THE ART OF DIRECTING THE FLOW

Magnetic passes are the "vibrational currents" that allow the practitioner to move from static observation to dynamic intervention. This chapter has demonstrated that your hands do not just feel; they direct, distribute, and harmonize the **Unity of Life (UL)** within the consultant's field. Mastery of these gestures is what transforms a simple touch into a precise frequency therapy.

Key Takeaways for Your Practice:

1. **The Hand as a Vector:** Your hands act as magnetic poles. Whether you are using **Transverse Passes** to clear blockages or **Longitudinal Passes** to restore circulation, your movement must be an extension of your focused intention.
2. **Rhythm and Fluidity:** The effectiveness of a pass lies in its regularity. A jerky or hesitant movement creates "vibrational noise." Aim for a fluid, constant motion that mirrors the natural rhythm of a calm breath.
3. **The Polarity Principle:** Remember that you are working with the body's natural polarities. By directing the flow from the head to the feet, you encourage grounding; by working from the center outward, you encourage expansion and release.

PRACTITIONER'S CHECKLIST: MASTERING THE PASSES

- **Cleansing (Transverse):** Did I use sharp, outward movements to "break" the surface densities?
- **Circulation (Longitudinal):** Did I follow the major energy channels to reconnect the upper and lower centers?
- **Centering (Circular):** Did I use slow, clockwise motions over the solar plexus or the heart to stabilize the new frequency?
- **The Zero Point Finish:** Did I end the sequence by returning to total stillness to let the consultant's system integrate the shift?

TRANSITION TO THE OPERATIONAL CORE:

The mastery of magnetic passes completes your technical "toolbox" for external intervention. You are now ready to enter the heart of the practice. In **Chapter 11 – Vibrational Transmission Protocols**, we will see how these gestures combine with your internal state to achieve a total **Frequency Transition**, moving from the "doing" of the pass to the "being" of the transmission.

"The hand suggests the movement, but the soul directs the destination. When the gesture is pure, the flow is unstoppable."

CHAPTER 11
VIBRATIONAL TRANSMISSION PROTOCOLS

This chapter constitutes the operational core of your practice. It defines how energy and information pass from the practitioner to the consultant through three distinct modalities.

Transmission is the act of transferring a coherent frequency toward a system in imbalance. In "Vibrational Transition," we do not give our own energy; we serve as a bridge so that the consultant can align with a restoration frequency. This chapter details the three modes of transmission that make you a complete practitioner.

A. TRANSMISSION BY MANUAL CONTACT (Conscious Touch)

Touch is the most direct conductor for vibration. The hand is not merely an emitter; it is an interface that merges with the consultant's field.

Conscious Touch: Unlike massage, which acts on the muscle, vibrational touch "listens" to the cell. The hand rests with the lightness of a feather but with the presence of a rock.

The Protocol:

- **Establishing contact**: Place your hands on the area to be treated (often the plexus, shoulders, or feet).
- **Merging**: Breathe at the same rhythm as the consultant. Feel the boundary between your hand and their body disappear.
- **Transmission**: Let the "Transition" frequency circulate. Do not push. Simply let the information of fluidity flow.

The Sensation : You will often feel a "suction" (the consultant's body calling for energy) followed by "repletion" (the tissue filling with heat and light). This is the sign that the transmission is complete in that area.

After learning to modulate through the mind (Part II) and to use magnetic passes (Chapter 10), we now approach Direct Transmission. This is the art of passing the Life Unit (LU) information through the skin barrier.

Conscious touch is not a massage. It is an interface communication. Where massage seeks to mobilize tissues through mechanical force, vibrational touch seeks to mobilize information through presence.

1. The Hand as a "Bio-Adapter"

Your hand serves as a transformer. It takes universal energy (the LU), colors it with your healing intention, and adapts it to the "voltage" that the consultant's body can accept.

- **Contact is not pressure**: In this protocol, the hand carries no weight. It rests like a leaf on the water.
- **Awareness of "Micro-Movement"**: Beneath a still hand, everything moves. Conscious touch allows you to perceive the fluidic and vibrational micro-movements that are invisible to the naked eye.

2. The 3 Keys to Conscious Touch

For a hand to truly transmit a healing frequency, it must integrate three technical parameters:

A. Transparency (The Manual Zero Point)

The hand must "want" nothing. If your hand is tensed by the desire to heal, it becomes an obstacle.

- Technique: Imagine that your hands are hollow. The energy does not come from your muscles; it flows through your arms from your central axis and exits through the center of your palms (the Laogong points).

B. Synchronization (Entrainment)

Before transmitting anything, you must "tune" yourself to the consultant's frequency.

- Exercise: Place your hand. Do nothing for 30 seconds. Wait to feel the heart or respiratory rhythm of the area. Once you "feel" the tissue, you can begin the transmission.

C. The Information Vector

This is where intention (Chapter 5) meets the gesture.

- While your hand touches the skin, your mind projects the information through the hand.
- Example: For a burn, the hand is cool and still. For devitalization, the hand is vibrant and warm.

3. PROTOCOL: Cellular Impregnation through Contact

This protocol is used to re-inform an organ or a traumatized area.

- **The Approach**: Enter the thermal field (at 2 cm) before touching the skin. Ask for energetic permission.
- **The Contact**: Place the entire palm. Avoid "pointed" fingers, which can be perceived as aggressive.
- **The "Pump" Phase**: Without moving the hand, visualize a flow entering the consultant's body on the inhale and diffusing into their tissues on the exhale.
- **The Withdrawal**: This is the most important phase. Withdraw your hand very slowly, as if you were peeling yourself away from a sticky substance. A sudden withdrawal creates a "vacuum shock" for the consultant.

4. PRACTITIONER'S ADVICE: Managing Heat

You will often notice your hands becoming burning hot. This is not your body temperature rising; it is the friction of high-frequency energy in your channels.

- **If the heat is pleasant**: Continue; this is a transmission of vitality.
- **If the heat becomes "stinging" or electrical**: You are reaching saturation. Withdraw your hands, shake them toward the earth, and perform a transverse pass to disperse the surplus.

B. MENTALIZED TRANSITION (At a Distance or Through Intention)

Vibration is not limited by space. Since we work on the informational plane (similar to radio waves), physical distance matters little if the intention is clear.

- **The Mechanism**: The practitioner's mind creates a "vibrational representation" of the consultant. By acting on this representation with an intention of neutrality and coherence, the consultant's actual field is modified via resonance (form-generating field).
- **The Protocol**:
  1. **Holographic Visualization**: Represent the consultant in front of you, or simply visualize their Unity of Life as a luminous sphere.
  2. **Zero Point**: Connect to your own center.
  3. **Emission:** Project the Transition information (e.g., "Calm," "Alignment") toward the representation. Hold this image steady until you feel a change in density in your own hands (the vibrational echo).
- **Usage**: Ideal for remote sessions or for acting on a person who cannot be touched (extreme pain, burns).

It is crucial to understand that Vibrational Transition knows no spatial barriers. If the body-instrument is the antenna, intention is the radio wave. Mentalized transmission rests on the principle of **non-locality**: healing information can be transmitted instantaneously, whether the consultant is inches or thousands of miles away.

1. The Mechanism of Vibrational Entanglement

When working mentally, you do not "travel" to the other person. You create a shared space of resonance.

- **Phasing**: Through focused thought, you tune your own field to the consultant's frequency.
- **Information Transfer**: Once the connection is established, you modulate your own internal state. Through a mirror effect, the consultant's energy system aligns with the coherence you maintain.

2. Mentalized Transmission Protocols

Working without hands requires rigorous mental discipline. There are three levels of application:

A. Proximity Radiance (Healing through the Field)

You are with the consultant but do not use your hands. Your aura acts as the broadcaster.

- **Technique**: Expand your energy field until it encompasses the consultant's. Maintain an intention of "Total Peace."
- **Utility**: Ideal for people in shock, burn victims, or highly agitated children.

B. Active Visualization (Etheric Surgery)

Mentally act on a specific structure (an organ, a vertebra) by "seeing" the information transform.

- **Protocol**: Visualize the organ in 3D. Observe its current color and density. Through intention, project a "Restore" frequency until the mental image becomes vibrant and luminous.

C. Remote Transmission (Out-of-Space Healing)

- **The Witness**: Use a support (name, photo, or precise visualization) to stabilize the target of your intention.
- **The Bridge**: Link your central Axis to the witness. Emit the required frequency (e.g., Recovery, Soothing).
- **Sealing**: It is imperative to break the mental connection at the end of the session to avoid remaining "entangled" with the consultant.

3. The Triad of Mentalized Effectiveness

- **Signal Clarity**: Your mental image must be sharp. A fuzzy thought yields a fuzzy result.
- **Effortlessness**: Do not "push" with your brain. Intention is emitted from the Heart (emotional engine) and directed by the Third Eye (rudder).
- **Certainty (Technical Faith)**: Act as if the modification is already accomplished. Doubt acts as interference.

4. PRACTITIONER'S ADVICE: Managing Mental Exhaustion

Mentalized transmission fatigues the nervous system more than manual magnetism.

- Limit intense focus to 15–20 minutes.
- **Return to the body**: After a remote session, drink water and walk barefoot or touch dense matter (wood, stone) to "disconnect" from the astral and return to your incarnation.

C. EMERGENCY DIFFUSION (Intervention in Case of Crisis)

In a crisis (emotional shock, panic, searing pain), the practitioner must act fast to prevent the collapse of the Unity of Life.

- **The Objective**: Stop immediate energy leakage and return the nervous system to parasympathetic mode.
- **The "Flash" Protocol**:
    1. **Lightning Recentering**: Recenter yourself in one second (deep grounding).
    2. **The Impact**: Place one hand on the forehead (calm the mind) and one on the solar plexus (calm the emotion).
    3. **The "Anchor" Frequency**: Emit a very low, heavy vibration to stop agitation. It is like dropping an anchor in a raging sea.
    4. **Hold**: Do not move until the consultant's breathing stabilizes or their eyes regain clarity.

1. The Law of the "Lighthouse in the Storm"

Your first tool is your **stability**. If you panic, you sink with them. You must become a pillar of immobility (**Absolute Zero Point**). Your internal calm is the reference frequency the consultant's system will align with to avoid "short-circuiting."

2. Rapid Intervention Protocols

A. The "Hot" Crisis (Inflammation, Burn, Anger, Panic)

There is an overflow of disordered energy. You must extract and cool.

- **Withdrawal Gesture**: Do not touch directly; work at 5 cm.
- **Intention**: "Absorption and Dispersion." Imagine your hands are frozen sponges.
- **Evacuation**: Flick your hands toward the ground frequently.

B. The "Cold" Crisis (Fainting, Shock, Stun, Exhaustion)

The system is disconnecting; energy is withdrawing inward. You must recall it to life and anchor it.

- **Strong Contact**: Firmly grasp the ankles, feet, or hands.
- **Intention**: "Recall and Presence." Call the Unity of Life back into the physical body.
- **Anchoring**: Visualize powerful roots going from the consultant's feet to the center of the earth.

3. The "Vibrational Compression" Technique

To stop an "energetic hemorrhage" (e.g., following a violent emotional shock):

- **Placement**: One hand on the solar plexus, the other on the back at the same level.
- **Action**: Exert psychic pressure (more than physical) to gather the scattering pieces of the field.
- **Breath**: Breathe slowly and audibly to force the consultant's system to sync with yours **(Respiratory Entrainment)**.

4. Limits of Intervention (Ethics Note)

- **Medical Emergency**: In case of cardiac distress or loss of consciousness, call emergency services (911/112) first. Vibrational transmission is a complement to stabilize shock, never a substitute.
- **Charge Transfer**: The risk of "absorbing" the other's pain is at its peak during emergencies. Maintain your shield: "I transmit Life; I do not take the ill."

SUMMARY FOR YOUR PRACTICE JOURNAL

- **Emergency** = Practitioner's Immobility. The more chaos in front of you, the more "stone-like" you must be.
- **Hot Crisis** = Disperse (Air/Water).
- **Cold Crisis** = Gather and Anchor (Earth).
- **The Word:** Use short, firm commands: "Breathe," "Return," "Here and now."

CONCLUSION OF CHAPTER 11

OPERATIONAL SYNTHESIS: FROM TECHNIQUE TO TRANSMISSION

Vibrational Transmission Protocols are not "recipes" to be followed mechanically; they are energetic frameworks designed to facilitate the shift from state A (Dissonance) to state B (Resonance). This chapter has shown you that the effectiveness of a protocol does not lie in the perfection of the gesture, but in the quality of the presence that inhabits it. You are no longer "doing" a treatment; you are "holding" a frequency.

Key Takeaways for Your Practice:

1. **Presence is the Primary Protocol:** No matter which specific sequence you choose—be it for trauma, physical pain, or emotional clearing—your own alignment at the **Zero Point** remains the engine of the transition. The protocol is the map, but your frequency is the vehicle.
2. **The Law of Minimal Effort:** In the new paradigm, results are not proportional to the force applied, but to the precision of the resonance. A single, well-timed frequency shift is more powerful than an hour of disorganized energetic manipulation.
3. **The Consultant as a Partner:** Every protocol is an invitation for the consultant's system to remember its own innate health. You are not "giving" something they lack; you are neutralizing the noise so their own **Life Unit (LU)** can sing again.

PRACTITIONER'S CHECKLIST: EVALUATING THE TRANSMISSION

- **Internal State:** Was I centered and neutral throughout the entire sequence?
- **Protocol Choice:** Did I select the protocol based on my **Informational Reading** rather than a mental diagnosis?
- **The Shift:** Did I wait for the "Vibrational Sigh" or the change in tissue density before moving to the next step?
- **Closing:** Did I properly seal the field to ensure the permanence of the new frequency?

TRANSITION TO MASTERY:

By mastering these protocols, you have moved from being a student of energy to a practitioner of Transition. However, to maintain this level of excellence, one must understand the subtle dynamics of the field. In Chapter 12 – Ethics, Posture, and Protection, we will explore how to remain a pure canal without becoming a sponge, ensuring your own sovereignty remains intact while you serve others.

"The protocol is the bridge, but the Love that flows through it is the destination. To transmit is to remind the other that they are already Whole."

CHAPTER 12
ETHICS AND PRACTITIONER POSTURE

Technical mastery (passes, tissue reading, modulation) is not enough to make a good Vibrational Transition practitioner. The quality of care depends primarily on the inner posture of the one providing it. In this chapter, we explore vibrational ethics: how to remain a pure, protected, and respectful channel.

A. BENEVOLENT NEUTRALITY: The Art of "Non-Willing"

The practitioner's greatest pitfall is the desire to heal. This may seem paradoxical, but "willing" is a mental tension that creates vibrational noise.

- **Do Not Be the Savior**: Desperately wanting the other person to get better injects your own will into their field. This can hinder their own transition.
- **Neutrality**: This is the "Zero Point" state. You are present and available, but without expectation of immediate results. You offer a frequency of coherence, and it is the consultant's body that chooses whether or not to embrace it.
- **Benevolence**: This is the soil that prevents neutrality from being cold. It is a space of unconditional welcome where the consultant feels safe enough to release their resistance.

Note: Neutrality is cultivated through the breath. If you feel yourself "pushing" with your mind, return to your grounding and exhale your will.

1. Why "Neutrality"?

If you "must" heal someone, you are no longer neutral. You inject your ego into the consultant's field.

- **The Risk**: Your will creates resistance. The consultant's body may subconsciously tense up against this intrusion.
- **The Solution**: Being neutral means accepting what is. You are the witness, not the savior.

2. Why "Benevolence"?

Neutrality alone could be cold and sterile. Benevolence is the vibrational lubricant.

- Heart Frequency: Benevolence emits a coherent wave that instantly soothes the consultant's amygdala (the fear center).

3. Establishing a Secure Framework for Transition

The effectiveness of a Vibrational Transition session does not depend on the "force" of the practitioner's will, but rather on the quality of the **vibrational container** they provide. Establishing a secure framework is the primary ethical duty of the practitioner.

1. **The Space of Non-Judgment:** A secure framework begins in the mind. The practitioner must welcome the consultant's "dissonances" (pain, emotional blocks, toxins) without labeling them as "bad." By remaining in a state of neutral observation, you prevent the consultant's system from going into a defensive contraction, which allows the cellular memory to surface safely.

2. **The Sovereignty of the Consultant:** The framework is secure because it respects the free will of the living system. We do not "force" a healing; we **propose** a coherent frequency. The practitioner must internalize the following: *"I offer the frequency of the Life Unit (LU), and the consultant's wisdom chooses what to integrate."* This posture removes the pressure of "result-seeking" and protects both parties from energetic exhaustion.
3. **Energetic Hermeticism:** A professional framework requires clear boundaries. As a practitioner, you are a "translucent canal," not a sponge.
   - **Before the session:** Clearly define the start of the transition through your centering ritual.
   - **During the session:** Maintain the "Zero Point" posture to avoid "taking on" the consultant's charges.
   - **After the session:** Formally close the field to ensure that no residual information remains linked to your own personal energy field.
4. **The Contract of Presence:** Security is felt through the stability of your presence. If your mind wanders, the "vibrational bridge" breaks. Establishing a secure framework means committing to total presence—where your breathing, your hands, and your intention are perfectly synchronized for the duration of the care.

Ethics Note: The practitioner is the guardian of the frequency. Your primary responsibility is to maintain your own high vibrational state so that the framework remains a sanctuary of transformation.

B. THE MECHANISM OF "NON-DOING" (WU WEI)

For the practitioner, benevolent neutrality translates into the concept of Non-Doing. It is not about doing nothing; it is about letting the action happen through you.

- **The Neutral Observer**: While your hands work, a part of your consciousness observes the scene as if from the outside.
- **Absence of Judgment**: Whether you perceive a charge of anger, sadness, or a heavy pathology, your frequency must remain stable. If you judge ("Oh, this is serious" or "This is dirty"), you lower your own frequency and saturate yourself with the consultant's information.

Training Exercise: "The Tree and the Waterfall"

- **The Tree (Grounding)**: Your legs and pelvis are immobile and solid. This is your neutrality.
- **The Waterfall (Benevolence)**: Your heart and hands let energy flow without restraint. This is your benevolence.
- Practice this state before every session: be solid like the tree, fluid like the water.

C. ETHICS AND RESPONSIBILITY

- **Respect for Freedom**: If the consultant's soul is not ready for the transition, you must respect that. We do not heal someone "in spite of themselves."
- **Humility of the Channel**: Never claim ownership of a successful treatment. You were the modulator, but it was the consultant's Unity of Life that performed the transformation.
- **Vibrational Confidentiality**: What you read in the tissues or memories is sacred. It must never leave the healing space.

D. MANAGING YOUR OWN ENERGY AFTER A SESSION

Every vibrational interaction leaves a trace. To manage your energy is to ensure your informational decontamination.

1. The "Sponge-Pathy" Syndrome

Many beginners finish their days exhausted. This is a technical error caused by:

- Unbroken Links: Remaining plugged into the consultant's frequency.
- Resonance Transfer: Your own field was too porous, absorbing the charge instead of letting it pass through to the earth.

2. Disconnection and Cleaning Protocols

- **A. The Break Gesture (The "Guillotine" Gesture)**: Cross your hands in a sharp "cutting" motion in front of your solar plexus while exhaling loudly. Intention: "What belongs to them stays with them; what belongs to me stays with me."
- **B. Discharge by the Elements**:
  - **Water**: Wash hands and forearms in cold water to carry away residual magnetic charges.
  - **Earth**: Walk barefoot or visualize roots evacuating "grey" energy to the earth's core.
  - **Fire**: Use a candle or incense (sage, palo santo) to "burn" stagnant miasmas in the room.

3. Recovering Vital Capital

- **The "Light Shower"**: For two minutes, visualize a column of white light filling your central channel.
- **Hara Centering**: Bring attention 3 cm below the navel (your battery) and breathe there until you feel warmth and fullness.

4. Workplace Hygiene: Maintaining the Sanctity of the Space

Just as a surgeon sterilizes their instruments between operations, the vibrational practitioner must "reset" the energy of their workspace. Information is volatile; if it is not cleared, the residues of a previous session can interfere with the next consultant's field.

1. Physical and Energetic Aeration

The first step in workplace hygiene is the movement of air.

- **The Action:** Open windows between each session, even for a few minutes.
- **The Principle:** Oxygen carries a high-frequency charge. By renewing the air, you physically displace the "gas toxins" (emotional residues) that may have been released during the treatment.

2. Neutralizing the Treatment Table

The surface where the consultant lies acts as a temporary storage for the densities that have been evacuated.

- **The Technique:** Beyond changing the sheets or protective covers, perform a quick **Transverse Pass** over the table.
- **The Intention:** "I release and ground all residual information from the previous session."

3. Using the Elements: Water and Salt

Water is a natural frequency absorber.

- **For the Practitioner:** Wash your hands and forearms with cold water up to the elbows after every session. This "breaks" the magnetic link and discharges any static buildup.
- **For the Room:** Placing a bowl of salt water in a corner or using high-quality incense/essential oils (like Cedar or Sage) helps maintain a high vibrational threshold.

4. The "Zero Point" Reset of the Room

Before welcoming a new person, stand in the center of your workspace.

- **The Visualization:** See a wave of white light expanding from the center of the room to the walls, dissolving any "grayness" or lingering emotional imprints.
- **The Goal:** To ensure that every new consultant enters a **Neutral Field**, free from the history of those who came before.

Practitioner's Note: A clean workplace is a sign of respect for the Divine Life Unit. It ensures that you, the practitioner, remain in a pristine environment that supports your own health while providing the highest quality of care.

E. SETTING A SECURE FRAMEWORK FOR TRANSITION

The "framework" is a vibrational container. For a consultant to drop their armor, they must feel they are in a "sacred" (protected and dedicated) environment.

1. The "Healing Bubble" (Vibrational Framework)

Before the consultant enters, "inform" the space. Visualize the room saturated with a frequency of safety and clarity.

2. Informed Consent

Explain briefly what you will do (contact or not, heat/cold sensations). Ask: "Do I have your permission to work on your field today?" This opens the doors of the etheric body.

3. Postural Stability

Your silence is often more therapeutic than your words. Keep your voice calm and your gestures slow.

4. Sensory Environment

Use dim lighting (Alpha waves) and ensure the room is warm—a cold body locks its tissues.

5. Handling Outbursts

During an emotional release (crying, shaking), never break contact abruptly. Stay present, breathe with them, and say: "It is coming out; you are safe."

SUMMARY FOR YOUR PRACTICE JOURNAL

- **Neutrality** = I do not judge, I expect nothing (The Rudder).
- **Benevolence** = I offer a space of safety and love (The Fuel).
- **Posture** = I am a channel, not the source of energy.
- **After each session**: Cut the link (Gesture) + Wash (Water) + Ventilate (Space).

CONCLUSION OF CHAPTER 12

OPERATIONAL SYNTHESIS: THE SOVEREIGNTY OF THE CANAL

The practitioner's posture is not a moral constraint, but a vibrational necessity. This chapter has established that your effectiveness is strictly proportional to your ability to remain a "pure canal." Ethics in Vibrational Transition is the art of serving the other without ever losing oneself. By mastering your alignment and your energetic boundaries, you ensure that the session remains a space of resonance and not one of exhaustion.

Key Takeaways for Your Practice:

1. **Protection through Frequency:** You do not protect yourself by building "walls," which only create separation and fear. You protect yourself by raising your frequency. A high and stable vibration is naturally hermetic to lower dissonant frequencies.
2. **The Non-Doing (Wu-Wei):** The greatest trap for a practitioner is the "will to heal." When you *want* a result, you leave your Neutrality and enter into a power struggle with the consultant's pathology. True transition occurs when you step aside and let the **Zero Point** act.
3. **Vibrational Hygiene:** Just as you wash your hands, you must "wash" your field. Use the grounding and clearing techniques after every session to return to your own **Sovereign Signature**.

PRACTITIONER'S CHECKLIST: POSTURE AND ETHICS

- **Neutrality:** Did I remain a "Silent Witness" without judging the consultant's state or history?
- **Non-Interference:** Did I respect the consultant's rhythm without trying to "force" a transition?

- **Sovereignty:** Am I still in my own axis, or have I absorbed the emotional "smog" of the session?
- **Accountability:** Did I remember that I am a facilitator, and that the consultant remains the sole master of their own healing process?

TRANSITION TO MASTERY:

With a solid ethical foundation and a mastered posture, you are now ready for the final technical stage. Now that you know how to remain stable, we will explore how to intentionally "tune" the field like a precision instrument. In Chapter 13 – Mastering Modulation, we will study how to shift between specific frequencies to address the targeted needs of the Life Unit.

"To be a practitioner is to be a stable shore for another's storm. The shore does not move; it simply provides the ground where the wave can finally rest."

PART V: LIVING THE TRANSITION DAILY

CHAPTER 13: MASTERING MODULATION

This text marks the transition from professional practice in the office to self-mastery within the world's turmoil. It teaches how to stop being a victim of surrounding frequencies and become a conscious, adaptable emitter.

Vibrational Transition is not a practice reserved for a treatment table or a meditation mat. Its true power is revealed in your ability to remain sovereign in the midst of chaos. Mastering modulation is the art of adjusting your "frequency slider" based on what life demands of you, without ever losing your axis.

A. ADAPTING YOUR FREQUENCY TO LIFE'S CHALLENGES

Every day, we cross different vibrational "climates": the aggression of a traffic jam, the density of a business meeting, or the lightness of a moment with friends. Most people are subject to these climates, and their Unity of Life (UV) rides a rollercoaster.

1. Frequential Flexibility

Mastering your vibration doesn't mean always being "high" in frequency. It means knowing how to descend into a frequency of density and strength to face a difficulty, or rise into a frequency of subtlety and openness to create.

2. The Law of Adaptation

The "Transitor" does not fight against the low frequencies of their environment. They modulate their own emission to become "transparent" to frequencies that do not serve them, or to positively influence the space by their presence alone.

3. The Warning Signal

Learn to detect the exact moment your frequency begins to align by mimicry with a toxic environment (clenching hands, short breath, critical thoughts). This is the signal that modulation is required.

In previous chapters, you learned to modulate for others. Now, you must learn to modulate for your own life path. Suffering often arises from a mismatch: using a frequency of anger to solve a problem that requires compassion, or a frequency of flight for a situation that requires grounding.

1. Frequential Reading of the Event

Every challenge (conflict, grief, career change) has a vibrational signature:

- **The "Lead"** Challenge (Heavy, blocked): Requires a modulation toward Fluidity.
- **The "Electric" Challenge (Stress, urgency)**: Requires a modulation toward Depth/Calm.
- **The "Fog" Challenge (Confusion)**: Requires a modulation toward Verticality.

2. The 3 Levers of Adaptation

To change frequency in seconds, use these internal levers:

- **A. The Respiratory Lever**: The breath is the frequency selector. To calm down (lower frequency), lengthen the exhale. To energize (raise frequency), emphasize the inhale and air retention.
- **B. The Attention Lever (Focus)**: Energy goes where attention flows. If your focus is on your Central Axis, you vibrate at your own frequency. The challenge becomes external information rather than an internal invasion.
- **C. The Verbal Lever (The Command)**: Use vibrational keywords to "lock in" a frequency. Pronounce internally: "Peace," "Solidity," "Openness."

B. THEMED RECENTERING
(Stress, Creativity, Relationships)

Themed Recentering is a specific modulation of your axis to meet a precise need.

1. Modulation against Stress (The "Earth-Calm" Frequency)

Stress is not just a psychological state; it is a high-pitched, erratic, and fragmented vibrational signature. When a consultant is under stress, their "Life Unit" (LU) is scattered at the periphery of their field. The practitioner's role is to act as a **tuning fork** to bring this energy back to a stable, low-frequency base: the **"Earth-Calm"** frequency.

- **The Signature of Stress:** A jagged, rapid wave. It manifests as mental "noise," shallow breathing, and muscular tension (the "armor" effect).
- **The Modulator's Objective:** To replace this "noise" with a deep, rhythmic, and grounding frequency that re-anchors the consciousness into the physical body.

The Protocol: "The Anchored Descent"

1. **Phase 1: Harmonic Entrainment**
    - Place your hands at a distance (20 cm) from the consultant's shoulders.
    - Do not try to "calm" them with your will. Instead, modulate your own internal frequency to a deep, slow rhythm (6 breaths per minute).
    - By resonance, the consultant's nervous system will begin to synchronize with your stability.
2. **Phase 2: The Earth-Calm Frequency**
    - Visualize a deep, moss-green or ochre light.
    - Project the information of **"Gravity and Safety."** Imagine this frequency as a dense, warm liquid flowing from the head down to the soles of the feet.
3. **Phase 3: The Solar Plexus Reset**
    - Apply a very light touch to the solar plexus.

- **The Intention:** *"The alert is over. You are safe within your structure."*
- Feel the "thaw" of the tissues under your palm as the stress-contraction dissolves.

The Sensation (Signs of Success):
You will know the modulation is successful when the consultant experiences a **spontaneous deep sigh** or a sudden heaviness in the limbs. The field, which was "bristling" and sharp, becomes smooth, soft, and silent.

Training Note: You cannot modulate stress if you are stressed yourself. Your primary tool is your own **grounding**. The more you are "Earth," the more the consultant can leave their "Storm."

2. Modulation for Creativity (The "Heaven-Opening" Frequency)

Creativity, in the sense of *Vibrational Transition*, is the ability of the human system to receive and interpret new information from the field of infinite possibilities. When a consultant feels "blocked" or "dry," it is often because their upper centers (the crown and third eye) are constricted or "grayed out" by mental repetition.

- **The Signature of Blockage:** A static, circular, and dense frequency. It feels like a "ceiling" of lead over the head, preventing the circulation of the Life Unit (LU) toward higher intuition.
- **The Modulator's Objective:** To create a "vibrational breach" in this ceiling and establish a vertical connection to the **"Heaven-Opening"** frequency—a state of pure receptivity and sparkling clarity.

The Protocol: "The Crystalline Aperture"

1. **Phase 1: Clearing the Mental Casing**
    - Place your hands at a distance (15 cm) on either side of the consultant's temples.
    - **The Intention:** *"I dissolve the mental static."*
    - Perform a slow, outward "opening" gesture with your palms, as if parting heavy curtains to reveal a clear sky.
2. **Phase 2: The Heaven-Opening Frequency**
    - Visualize a brilliant, iridescent white or pale violet light.
    - **The Modulation:** Generate a very high, fine, and "sparkling" frequency. Imagine the sound of a crystal bell.
    - Project this frequency toward the **Crown Chakra**. Feel the field becoming lighter, more "porous," and infinitely vast.
3. **Phase 3: Informational Fluidity**
    - Move one hand to the base of the skull (occiput) and the other above the forehead.

- **The Command:** "Allow the flow of new ideas. Restore verticality."
- Feel the energy begin to circulate in a vertical "loop," connecting the Earth to the Sky through the central canal.

The Sensation (Signs of Success):
The consultant may experience a sensation of "cool air" on the scalp, a sudden widening of their internal vision, or a feeling of "floating" lightness. The mental pressure vanishes, replaced by a sense of **joyful curiosity**.

Training Note: This modulation is particularly effective for artists, entrepreneurs, or anyone facing a life transition that requires "seeing beyond" current limitations. You are not giving them ideas; you are **cleaning the antenna** so they can receive their own.

3. Relational Modulation (The "Heart-Radiance" Frequency)

Relational difficulties—whether they stem from a recent conflict, a lack of self-love, or the "energetic cords" of a toxic attachment—always manifest as a constriction of the chest area. In *Vibrational Transition*, we understand that a "closed" heart is a heart whose frequency has become defensive, rigid, and retracted.

- **The Signature of Contraction:** A dense, gray, or "thorny" vibration around the sternum. It feels like a protective shield that has become a prison, preventing the Life Unit (LU) from radiating outward.
- **The Modulator's Objective:** To dissolve the "armor" and restore the **"Heart-Radiance"** frequency—a state of warm, expansive, and compassionate presence.

The Protocol: "The Compassionate Expansion"

1. **Phase 1: Softening the Shield**
    - Place your hands at a distance (10 cm) in front of and behind the Heart Chakra (center of the chest and between the shoulder blades).
    - **The Intention:** *"I acknowledge the protection, but I authorize the softening."*
    - Generate a frequency of **"Tenderness"** (a warm, pink, or golden-rose light). Feel the density of the "shield" beginning to melt like wax.
2. **Phase 2: Activating Heart-Radiance**
    - Move your hands slightly further apart as the field expands.
    - **The Modulation:** Project the information of **"Unconditional Acceptance."** Visualize the heart center as a sun that begins to shine through the clouds.
    - The frequency should feel like a "warm embrace"—broad, inclusive, and rhythmic.
3. **Phase 3: Harmonizing the Cords**

- Use your fingers as "vibrational combs" to smooth the energy lines leaving the heart toward the outside.
- **The Command:** "Release the hooks. Restore the purity of the link."
- Feel the "pulling" sensations vanish, replaced by a sense of **internal fullness**.

The Sensation (Signs of Success):
The consultant often experiences a "warm wave" spreading through the arms and face. Breathing becomes involuntary and deep. There is a shift from "I am against" to "I am," marked by a profound sense of **peaceful connection**.

Training Note: You cannot modulate the heart of another if you are in judgment. To succeed, you must first connect to your own "Heart-Radiance." You are not "fixing" their relationship; you are **reminding their heart** of its natural capacity to love and be loved.

4. TRAINING EXERCISE: The Crowd Test

Objective: To maintain your Sovereign Frequency and your "Zero Point" while immersed in a chaotic or high-density emotional environment. This is the ultimate test for the practitioner's stability.

In the silence of a treatment room, modulation is easy. In a crowd (a busy street, a subway, a shopping mall), the collective "noise" tends to pull your frequency toward the average—often a state of stress, haste, or fatigue.

The Protocol: "The Pillar in the Current"

1. **Phase 1: Internal Anchoring (Before Entering)**
    - Before entering a crowded space, stop for a moment.
    - Close your eyes and activate your **"Earth-Calm"** frequency.
    - Feel your vertical axis (the silver thread) connecting the center of the Earth to the Crown.
    - **The Affirmation:** *"I am the observer. My field is hermetic and luminous."*
2. **Phase 2: Intentional Immersion**
    - Walk into the crowd. Do not look at the ground; keep your gaze horizontal and "soft" (panoramic vision).
    - Notice the "vibrational waves" of the people around you without absorbing them. See them as passing clouds.
    - **The Modulation:** Intentionally emit a frequency of **"Silent Peace."** Imagine that your aura is a golden bubble that smooths the air 2 meters around you as you move.
3. **Phase 3: The Transparency Test**
    - If you feel a "bump" (someone's anger, a sudden noise, a push), do not contract.

- **The Technique:** Become "transparent." Let the dissonance pass *through* your field without finding anything to hook onto.
- Return instantly to your breath.

The Feedback (Signs of Success):

- **External:** You will notice that people spontaneously give you more space, or that the path seems to "open up" naturally before you.
- **Internal:** You exit the crowd with the same level of energy (Life Unit) as when you entered, without feeling "drained" or agitated.

Mastery Note: This exercise transforms the world into your laboratory. When you can maintain your "Heart-Radiance" or "Earth-Calm" in the middle of a terminal or a market, you have truly mastered modulation. You are no longer a victim of the environment; you are a **frequency transmitter**.

C. FREQUENCY CHANGE PROTOCOL (The A.S.I. Method)

To switch from one theme to another in under 60 seconds, use the A.S.I. method:

1. **A. Arrest**: Pause physically. Stop all movement.
2. **S. Step-Breath** : Take three deep breaths targeting the specific center (Belly for stress, Heart for relationships, Head for creativity).
3. **I. Intention**: Formulate the internal command corresponding to the new desired frequency.

The "Craft" of Living

The practitioner must not wait to be in their office to practice:

- In a queue (Stress) $\rightarrow$ Practice **Grounding.**
- Listening to a friend (Relationships) $\rightarrow$ Practice **Heart Coherence.**
- Cooking (Creativity) $\rightarrow$ Practice **Expansion**.

Every moment becomes a micro-session of Transition. This constant practice makes your central channel invulnerable to the fluctuations of the outside world.

1. Stress Theme: The "Earth-Grounding" Modulation

When the human system is under chronic stress, it operates in a "high-voltage" state. The frequency is rapid, superficial, and disconnected from the lower body. This protocol is designed to perform a **forced grounding**—not by struggling against the stress, but by offering a magnetic "anchor" that pulls the excess energy back into the earth.

- **The Signature of Stress:** A high-pitched, electric, and fragmented vibration. It accumulates in the head, jaw, and shoulders.
- **The Modulator's Objective:** To apply the **"Earth-Grounding"** frequency—a low, dense, and rhythmic vibration that restores the connection between the base of the spine and the ground.

The 4-Step Technical Protocol

1. **The "Shock Absorber" Contact**

- **Action:** Place one hand on the **occiput** (base of the skull) and the other on the **sacrum** (base of the spine).
- **The Mental Posture:** Do not "push" the energy. Simply act as a conductor.
- **Frequency:** Generate a deep, muffled "hum" internally. Visualize the color of wet clay or dark granite.

2. The Downward Polarization

- **Action:** While maintaining the hand on the sacrum, move the upper hand slowly down the spine.
- **The Intention:** "I drain the excess voltage."
- **Visualization:** Imagine your hand is a magnet pulling a heavy, metallic liquid from the brain down toward the tailbone.

3. Earth-Grounding Injection

- **Action:** Place both hands on the consultant's feet (or over the ankles if the person is lying down).
- **The Command:** "Anchor. Stabilize. Ground."
- **The Modulation:** Emit a frequency of **absolute stillness**. Feel the weight of the consultant's legs increase as they reconnect with the planet's gravity.

4. The "Root" Seal

- **Action:** Visualize energetic roots extending from the consultant's feet and coccyx, deep into the soil.
- **The Goal:** To ensure the Life Unit (LU) is no longer "floating" but is firmly seated in the physical structure.

The Sensation (Signs of Success):
The consultant's breathing will shift from the chest to the abdomen. You will feel the "electric" buzzing in the field disappear, replaced by a **dense and warm silence**. The skin often changes color slightly (becoming less pale) as the blood flow returns to the extremities.

Mastery Note: This protocol is a "vibrational reset." It is particularly effective for anxiety attacks or mental exhaustion. By grounding the frequency, you allow the consultant to regain their **Sovereignty** over their own biological system.

2. Creativity Theme: The "Air-Expansion" Modulation

When the creative process is stalled, the human vibrational field often appears "compacted." The mental body is hyper-active but locked in a closed loop, creating a frequency of density and "grayness" around the head and throat. The **"Air-Expansion"** modulation is designed to break this compression by introducing a high, light, and multidimensional frequency that allows the Life Unit (LU) to breathe again.

- **The Signature of Stagnation:** A heavy, repetitive, and low-amplitude vibration. It feels like "thick fog" or a leaden weight in the frontal lobe and the throat chakra.

- **The Modulator's Objective:** To apply the **"Air-Expansion"** frequency—a crystalline, rapid, and expansive vibration that restores the vertical connection to the "Field of All Possibilities."

The 4-Step Technical Protocol

1. **The "Cloud-Breaker" Opening**
    - **Action:** Place your hands 10 cm away from the consultant's temples, palms facing inward.
    - **The Mental Posture:** Do not focus on the "problem." Focus on the "space" between the molecules.
    - **Frequency:** Generate a vibration of **"Iridescence."** Visualize a breeze clearing a heavy mist.
2. **The Throat-Crown Alignment**
    - **Action:** Place one hand over the throat chakra (without contact) and the other above the crown.
    - **The Intention:** "I restore the bridge between Expression and Inspiration."
    - **Visualization:** Imagine a vertical shaft of sapphire-blue light connecting the voice to the higher mind, removing any "knots" of doubt or self-censorship.
3. **Air-Expansion Projection**
    - **Action:** Using a "fanning" motion with your hands, move from the center of the chest upward and outward beyond the head.
    - **The Command:** "Expand. Lighten. Receive."
    - **The Modulation:** Emit a frequency of **"Weightlessness."** Feel the field becoming porous, as if the consultant's aura is doubling in size and becoming filled with light.
4. **The "Spark" Anchor**
    - **Action:** Gently tap the "Third Eye" area (between the eyebrows) with your fingertips to "wake up" the pineal gland.
    - **The Goal:** To switch the brain from "linear-analytical" mode to "spherical-intuitive" mode.

The Sensation (Signs of Success):
The consultant will often report a feeling of "coolness" or "tingling" at the top of the head. Their eyes may brighten, and their posture will naturally straighten as the "weight" is lifted. The field, previously dense, now feels **effervescent and vast**.

Mastery Note: This protocol is not about *finding* an idea; it is about *becoming a vessel* for one. By changing the frequency to "Air-Expansion," you create the vacuum required for a "New Information" (the Spark) to rush in.

3. Relational Theme: The "Heart-Coherence" Modulation

In the context of relational stress—whether it involves a conflict with others or a lack of internal harmony—the heart center (Anahata) tends to "vibrate out of phase." Instead of a steady, expansive radiation, the field becomes irregular, defensive, and "spiky." The **"Heart-Coherence"** modulation is a precision tool used to re-establish a rhythmic, magnetic, and compassionate pulse within the consultant's Life Unit (LU).

- **The Signature of Discord:** A chaotic, "noisy," and retracted vibration. It feels like a cold knot in the center of the chest or a rigid barrier that prevents genuine exchange.
- **The Modulator's Objective:** To apply the **"Heart-Coherence"** frequency—a warm, rhythmic, and "golden" vibration that entrains the entire system into a state of emotional safety and resonance.

The 4-Step Technical Protocol

1. **The "Pulse-Sync" Contact**
   - **Action:** Place your dominant hand 5 cm above the center of the sternum and your other hand on the back, directly between the shoulder blades.
   - **The Mental Posture:** Become a "Silent Witness." Do not judge the pain; simply offer a stable shore for the wave to land on.
   - **Frequency:** Generate a frequency of **"Deep Softness."** Visualize a rose-gold light glowing between your two palms, passing through the heart.
2. **The Rhythmic Entrainment**
   - **Action:** Coordinate your own breathing with a slow, 5-second inhale and 5-second exhale.
   - **The Intention:** "I synchronize the rhythms. I restore the song of the heart."
   - **Visualization:** Imagine a metronome of light pulsing in the center of the chest, gradually smoothing out the "jagged edges" of the emotional field.
3. **Heart-Coherence Expansion**
   - **Action:** Slowly move your hands away from the body in a circular, blossoming motion.
   - **The Command:** "Radiate. Connect. Soften."
   - **The Modulation:** Emit a frequency of **"Luminous Warmth."** Feel the field opening up like a flower, moving from a defensive "closed" state to an "available" state.
4. **The "Unity" Seal**
   - **Action:** Place both hands briefly on the consultant's shoulders, applying a very light, grounding pressure.

- **The Goal:** To integrate the heart's new coherence into the physical structure, ensuring the person feels both "open" and "protected" simultaneously.

The Sensation (Signs of Success):

The consultant will often experience a "melting" sensation in the chest, followed by a spontaneous smile or a feeling of "coming home." The breathing becomes effortless and expansive. The field, which was "bristling," is now **smooth, magnetic, and inviting**.

Mastery Note: This protocol does not "fix" a relationship; it **realigns the individual** so they can interact from a place of sovereignty rather than reaction. By establishing "Heart-Coherence," you allow the consultant to move from the "frequency of the wound" to the **"frequency of the link."**

4. Frequency Change Protocol: The Mechanics of State-Shifting

To change the frequency of a living system is not an act of "willpower," but an act of **vibrational substitution**. As a practitioner of Transition, you do not fight the existing shadow; you introduce a light of a different quality that renders the shadow non-existent. This protocol is the formal sequence used to transition a consultant from a state of "Dissonance" (stagnation, pain, or noise) to a state of "Resonance" (flow, health, or silence).

The Foundation: The Law of Entrainment

The protocol relies on the physical principle of entrainment: when two oscillating systems are in proximity, the weaker or more chaotic one will naturally synchronize with the stronger, more coherent one.

The 5 Stages of the Universal Protocol:

1. **Phase 1: The Zero-Point Alignment (The Anchor)**
    - Before touching the consultant or their field, the practitioner must "empty" their own mental space.
    - **The Action:** Connect to your vertical axis. Become the "immovable rock." If you are not stable, you cannot act as a reference frequency.
2. **Phase 2: Resonance Capture (The Tuning)**
    - Place your hands in the field (Distal) to "feel" the current frequency.
    - **The Action:** Acknowledge the dissonance without judgment. Identify the "texture" of the blockage (Is it electric? Is it heavy? Is it cold?).
3. **Phase 3: Frequency Injection (The Transition)**
    - Begin to modulate your own internal state to the target frequency (Earth, Air, or Heart).
    - **The Action:** Use the **"Breathing Pump"**—inhale the universal Life Unit (LU) and exhale the new frequency through your palms into the consultant's centers.
4. **Phase 4: Stabilization (The Integration)**
    - Once you feel the "thaw" or the shift in the consultant's field, hold the position.

- **The Action:** Maintain the new frequency until the consultant's tissues begin to pulse in unison with your hands. This prevents the "rebound effect" where the system tries to return to its old, painful habit.

5. **Phase 5: The Sovereign Seal (The Closure)**
    - Gently withdraw your hands and visualize a "crystalline film" surrounding the new frequency.
    - **The Action:** Affirm internally: *"This new state is now the reference. The transition is complete."*

The Practitioner's Secret:
The speed of the frequency change is directly proportional to your **Neutrality**. The less you "try" to change the person, the faster the person changes. You are simply providing the high-definition "blueprint" of health, and the consultant's cells—starved for coherence—will naturally rush to adopt it.

Training Note: Practice this protocol on yourself first. Change your own frequency from "Tired" to "Vital" using these five steps. Only when you can shift your own state in under 60 seconds are you ready to guide another through the protocol.

5. Application in the "Profession" of Living

The mastery of modulation is not a skill reserved solely for the treatment room. It is a fundamental tool for the **"Profession" of Living**. In the philosophy of Vibrational Transition, we are not merely practitioners who "do" a session; we are vibrational beings who interact with the world through our frequency. This article explores how to apply the Frequency Change Protocol to the complexities of daily life.

- **The Living Practitioner:** You are your own primary consultant. Every challenge in your day—a difficult conversation, a moment of fatigue, a sudden fear—is an opportunity to apply a frequency shift.
- **The Objective:** To move from a "Reactive Life" (being a victim of external frequencies) to a "Sovereign Life" (being the conscious emitter of your own state).

The 3 Daily Modalities of the Protocol:

1. **The "Social Buffer" (Relational Application)**
    - **When:** During a conflict or in a high-tension meeting.
    - **The Action:** Apply the **"Heart-Coherence"** modulation internally. Do not wait for the other person to calm down.
    - **The Effect:** By stabilizing your own heart field, you create a "vibrational vacuum" that forces the surrounding tension to de-escalate. You become the silent anchor in the storm.
2. **The "Vitality Bridge" (Physical Application)**

- **When:** When you feel drained by your environment or "polluted" by collective stress.
- **The Action:** Use the **"Earth-Grounding"** protocol while standing or walking.
- **The Effect:** You discharge the static "noise" of the day and reconnect with the Earth's regenerative current. You learn to "empty" yourself in real-time rather than storing the charge.

3. **The "Visionary Shift" (Creative Application)**
   - **When:** When faced with a problem that seems to have no solution.
   - **The Action:** Step away and trigger the **"Air-Expansion"** modulation.
   - **The Effect:** You rise above the "density" of the problem. By changing your frequency, you allow a different quality of information (the "New Idea") to enter your field.

The Golden Rule: "Frequency First"
In the "Profession" of Living, the rule is simple: **Frequency precedes Action.** Before speaking, before deciding, before reacting—check your frequency. If you are in dissonance, any action you take will carry that dissonance. Use the 5-step protocol to reset to "Zero Point" first.

Final Training Note: The world does not need more "healers"; it needs more people who have mastered the art of being. When you live the Transition, your very presence becomes a protocol of healing for everyone you encounter. You no longer "work" at your practice; you **vibrate your truth**.

This concludes the technical and philosophical journey of Chapter 13. We have covered the theory of modulation, the themed recentering, and the formal change protocols.

CONCLUSION OF CHAPTER 13

OPERATIONAL SYNTHESIS: THE PRECISION OF THE TUNING FORK

Mastering modulation is the final stage of the practitioner's technical expertise. It marks the transition from "cleaning" a field to "tuning" it with intention. This chapter has demonstrated that you are not a passive observer, but an active resonance point. By choosing to emit a specific frequency—be it **Earth-Calm**, **Air-Expansion**, or **Heart-Coherence**—you offer the consultant's system a coherent blueprint to follow.

Key Takeaways for Your Practice:

1. **Substitution, Not Struggle:** You do not fight stress or blockage; you replace a dissonant frequency with a more coherent one. The lower frequency naturally yields to the higher, more stable one through the **Law of Entrainment**.
2. **The Internal Reference:** Your ability to modulate the consultant's field depends entirely on your ability to modulate your own. You must *become* the

frequency you wish to transmit. You are the tuning fork; the consultant is the string that begins to vibrate in unison.

3. **The Power of Themes:** Themed recentering (Stress, Creativity, Relations) allows for surgical precision in your work. By identifying the "vibrational color" of the imbalance, you can apply the exact frequency shift needed to restore the **Unity of Life (UL)**.

PRACTITIONER'S CHECKLIST: EVALUATING MODULATION

- **Initial Capture:** Did I clearly identify the signature of the dissonance (e.g., the "jaggedness" of stress)?
- **Internal Shift:** Did I successfully activate the target frequency (Earth, Air, or Heart) within my own axis?
- **The Merge:** Did I feel the consultant's field "soften" and adopt the new rhythm?
- **Stabilization:** Did I hold the modulation long enough for the new state to become the consultant's new reference point?

FINAL TRANSITION:

You have now mastered the tools, the protocols, the posture, and the modulation. You are equipped to navigate the complexities of the vibrational field. But beyond techniques lies the ultimate goal of this path: the stabilization of your own unique identity in the new paradigm. In the final chapter, Chapter 14 – The Sovereign Signature, we will explore how to live these principles permanently, turning the Transition into a state of being.

"The master does not play the instrument; they become the music. When your frequency is steady, the world around you has no choice but to harmonize."

CHAPTER 14: THE CONSCIOUS VIBRATIONAL BEING

We have reached the end of this journey—or rather, the threshold of a new way of existing. In the previous chapters, we learned to listen, to clean, to modulate, and to transmit. This final chapter is not an ending but a synthesis: how all these building blocks assemble to form what we now call the Conscious Vibrational Being.

A. THE SYNTHESIS: Toward Total Vibrational Autonomy

Autonomy is the ultimate goal of Vibrational Transition. To be autonomous is not to never need help again; it is to possess within yourself the compass and the tools to return to balance, regardless of external chaos.

- **The Integration of Skills**: Autonomy is born from the fusion of your acquired knowledge:
    - **Recentering** has become a reflex, a second nature that brings you back to your axis in a single breath.
    - **Body Reading** allows you to immediately identify a drop in your Unity of Life (UV) before it manifests as fatigue or illness.
    - **Modulation** allows you to stop being a victim of your environment and instead choose the frequency with which you interact with it.
- **The Stable Unity of Life**: The Vibrational Being no longer seeks to "raise" their vibration in an artificial or temporary way. They seek stability. Autonomy means maintaining a high and coherent vibrational plateau, creating a zone of safety around oneself.
- **The Tool-Free Approach at the Summit**: At this stage, you realize that the absence of tools (pendulums, crystals, supports) is not a lack, but a liberation. Your own structure has become the most precise instrument there is. You walk through the world being your own laboratory, your own healer.

Autonomy is validated when the practitioner no longer needs to consult their notes to act. The protocol has faded away to make room for a fluid presence.

1. Conclusion: Becoming the Master of Your Own Frequency

Becoming the master of your frequency is not about exercising rigid control over yourself; it is about entering into a conscious dance with Life.

- **Inner Sovereignty**: Being the master of your frequency means you have retaken the reins of your internal state. You understand that **Information** (thoughts, beliefs) commands **Energy**, and that Energy commands **Matter**. By changing the information at the source, you change your reality.
- **Service to the World**: As a Conscious Vibrational Being, your simple presence becomes an act of transition for others. Through the law of resonance, a centered and vibrant person involuntarily offers an anchor point to those around them. The "craft" of the Transitor then moves beyond the session and becomes a way of being.
- **The Last Word: Feeling**: If only one thing were to remain, let it be the feeling. Never believe what you read; believe what you feel. Truth lies in the

vibration of your tissues, in the heat of your palms, and in the clarity of your axis.

2. The Final Message

Conscious Vibrational Transition is an invitation to stop being a spectator of your biology and become the architect of your frequency. You are not a drop of water in the ocean; you are the entire ocean in a drop of water, vibrating with a thousand possible frequencies. Choose yours. Embody it. Live it.

3. From Learning Techniques to Embodying a State of Being

This final chapter is a beginning. After exploring purification, tissue reading, and transmission protocols, we must now unify this knowledge to reach the ultimate goal of Transition: **Autonomy**.

In this context, vibrational autonomy is not isolation. It is the ability to no longer depend on external conditions (or third-party practitioners) to maintain balance. It is becoming your own frequency modulator.

4. Moving Beyond the Duality of "Treatment vs. Daily Life"

Autonomy begins when you understand that the Unity of Life (UV) does not only activate on a massage table.

- **The Old Paradigm**: "I feel bad, I take a remedy or receive a treatment."
- **The Conscious Being Paradigm**: "I perceive a drop in frequency; I instantly readjust my axis and my breath to restore coherence."

  It is the shift from "repair mode" to "permanent preventive maintenance."

5. The Autonomy Triangulation

To stabilize this autonomy, the Conscious Vibrational Being relies on three pillars:

1. **Vigilance (The Radar)**: The ability to feel a contraction in the tissues or a cloud in the aura in real-time.
2. **Responsibility (The Choice)**: No longer blaming the environment for one's vibrational state, but choosing the frequency of the response.
3. **Mastery (The Action)**: Immediately applying the necessary micro-protocol (grounding, smoothing, or expansion).

6. Steps of Final Integration

A. **Egotic Transparency**: Total autonomy requires that the ego no longer seeks to "shine" or "save." The more transparent you are, the more the UV flows without resistance. You no longer perform the treatment; you are the treatment.

B. **Stability of the Central Channel**: Autonomy rests on the strength of your Tube of Light. If it is solid, external storms (social stress, electromagnetic waves) simply slide off your aura without ever penetrating your deep structure.

C. **Harmony with Cycles**: The autonomous being knows that their vibration is not linear. They accept phases of "low pressure" (cleaning) and "high pressure" (action). They do not fight their own cycles; they accompany them.

7. Global Vision: From Individual to Collective

When you reach this autonomy, you become a "**Point of Coherence**." By your simple presence, without even using your hands, you stabilize the vibrational field of the places you move through and the people you encounter. This is the highest form of the craft: **transmission through silent emanation**.

SUMMARY FOR YOUR PRACTICE JOURNAL

- **Autonomy** = Vigilance + Responsibility + Micro-adjustment.
- The goal is not perfection, but the ability to **return to the center quickly**.
- The ultimate tool is your own **conscious presence.**

B. THE MASTER OF THE SIGNAL

To conclude this journey is to pass from the status of a passenger to that of the pilot of your own vibrational vessel.

1. Frequential Sovereignty

Mastery means choosing, at every moment, the quality of presence you offer the world.

2. The Law of Least Effort

Healing and balance do not require force, but clarity. Do not "push" energy; simply remove the obstacles so the UV can do its natural work.

3. The Discipline of Joy

Joy is the highest and most protective frequency. Cultivating gratitude is a vibrational strategy to maintain high energetic immunity.

4.The Ethics of Transmission

You only ever transmit what you are. Your own alignment is your primary healing tool.

C. FINAL WORD: The Beginning of Practice

You have learned to:

- Identify blockages in matter and subtle bodies.
- Clear emotional charges and crystallized memories.
- Transmit coherent information through your hands and intention.
- Maintain your own axis in daily chaos.

FINAL SUMMARY FOR YOUR PRACTICE JOURNAL

- Mastery = Awareness + Technique + Love.
- The Goal = Embodying the Unity of Life in every cell.
- The Future = You are now a broadcaster of peace for the world.

CONCLUSION – CHAPTER 14

FINAL SYNTHESIS: EMBODYING THE NEW PARADIGM

Being a "Conscious Vibrational Being" is the ultimate destination of this journey. This final chapter has shown you that the protocols and techniques learned throughout this book are not just tools to be used occasionally, but steps toward a permanent state of consciousness. Transition is no longer an action you perform; it is the frequency from which you live, breathe, and interact with the world.

Key Takeaways for Your Sovereign Life:

1. **From Doing to Being:** The true power of the practitioner does not lie in the complexity of the gesture, but in the stability of their presence. When you embody your **Sovereign Signature**, your mere presence becomes a catalyst for balance in your environment.
2. **The Continuity of the Field:** You have learned that there is no separation between your "practice" and your "life." Every challenge is a vibrational invitation to return to the **Zero Point**, and every joy is an expansion of your **Life Unit (LU)**.
3. **The Responsibility of Radiance:** As a conscious being, you understand that your frequency contributes to the collective field. By maintaining your own alignment, you provide a reference point of health and harmony for the global transition.

THE PRACTITIONER'S FINAL OATH

- **I AM** the guardian of my own frequency.
- **I STAND** as a stable axis between Earth and Sky.
- **I SERVE** the life force by remaining a neutral and compassionate canal.
- **I RADIATE** the signature of the Solution, trusting that matter will always follow the vibration of Spirit.

CLOSING WORDS:

The manual ends here, but your mastery is just beginning. You are now equipped with the inner technology to navigate the frequencies of the new era. Remember: **Vibration precedes form.** By changing your frequency, you have already changed your world.

"The path of Transition is a return Home—to the space where you are already Whole, Sovereign, and Free. Walk this path with joy, for the Light you seek is the very Light you are emitting."

ANNEXES

THE PRACTITIONER'S PRACTICAL GUIDE

1. THE VIBRATIONAL PROTOCOL CHECKLIST

Use this as a mental roadmap before and during every session.

1. **Preparation (The Internal Anchor)**
    - Perform a 1-minute **Central Axis** alignment.
    - Set the **Zero Point** (Neutrality/Benevolence).
    - Inform the space (The "Healing Bubble").
2. **Assessment (The Reading)**
    - Scan the thermal field (2-5 cm from the body).
    - Identify "hot" zones (inflammation/congestion) or "cold" zones (voids/leaks).
    - Perform tissue listening through light manual contact.
3. **Action (The Transition)**
    - **Rupture**: Use transverse passes to break crystallized patterns.
    - **Impregnation**: Use palm impositions to nourish organs or centers.
    - **Circulation**: Use longitudinal passes to redistribute energy.
4. **Integration (The Closing)**
    - Harmonize the poles (Diagonal Bridge-Hands).
    - Seal the vertical axis (Sky-Earth balance).
    - **Disconnection**: Physical withdrawal and energetic "cut."

2. TECHNICAL REFERENCE TABLES

The Four Fundamental Gestures

Gesture	Primary Function	Element Association
Longitudinal Pass	Soothing, smoothing, global diffusion.	Water (Flow)
Transverse Pass	Breaking blockages, cutting ties, dispersing.	Air (Movement)
Imposition	Feeding, focusing, densifying energy.	Fire (Heat)
Bridge-Hands	Harmonizing, stabilizing, connecting poles.	Earth (Structure)

The Three Calibration Distances

Distance	Target Layer	Best For...
Contact	Physical Body / Organs	Chronic pain, physical trauma, devitalization.
5–10 cm	Etheric Body (Vitality)	General fatigue, localized inflammation.
20–30 cm	Emotional Body	Stress, anxiety, mental agitation, trauma.

3. FREQUENCY MODULATION COMMANDS

Internal "Keywords" to lock in your intention.

- **To Calm**: "Density... Stillness... Earth."
- **To Activate**: "Vibration... Light... Upward."

- **To Cleanse**: "Fluidity... Transparency... Flow."
- **To Protect**: "Sovereignty... Axis... Shield."

4. EMERGENCY INTERVENTION SUMMARY

- **For Acute Pain/Burns**: Maintain a distance of 5 cm. Visualize "Sponges of Ice." Use the Absorption and Dispersion technique.
- **For Panic Attacks**: One hand on the forehead, one on the solar plexus. Force a slow, audible respiratory rhythm (Respiratory Entrainment).
- **For Fainting/Shock**: Firm contact on the soles of the feet. Command: "Return. Anchor. Here and now."

5. POST-SESSION HYGIENE FOR THE PRATITIONER

1. **The "Guillotine" Cut**: A sharp, crossed-arm movement in front of the plexus to break the energetic link.
2. **Thermal Reset**: Wash hands and forearms with cold water.
3. **Grounding:** 2 minutes of walking barefoot or visualizing roots to discharge residual information.

A. SHEETS 1-7

📝 SHEET 1: Vibrational Lexicon and Glossary: Key Terms of Vibrational Transition.

To achieve authentic vibrational mastery, you must be able to clearly name what you perceive.

1. Complete Lexicon of the Essential Notions:

Fundamental Notions

- **Vibration**: The energetic frequency emitted by an organism, a thought, an emotion, or a place.
- **Frequency**: The speed of oscillation of an energy; the higher it is, the clearer and more stable it becomes.
- **Energetic Density**: A heavy, stagnant, or slow-moving charge, often linked to undigested emotions.
- **High-Frequency State**: Optimal energetic alignment, fostering clarity, intuition, and stability.

Techniques and Processes

- **Recentering**: Returning to the axis; the instantaneous harmonization of the mental, emotional, and energetic bodies.
- **Neutralization**: The dissolution of disruptive or toxic energies.
- **Transmutation**: The transformation of a low energy into a rebalanced energy.
- **Vibrational Transmission**: The voluntary emission of energy, through intention or channeling.

Advanced Concepts

- **Life Matrix**: The informational grid that structures energetic organization.
- **Vibrational Coherence**: The alignment of intentions, thoughts, emotions, and actions.
- **Intuitive Expansion**: The opening, clarity, and amplification of subtle perception.
- **Inner Line**: Natural and stable vibrational guidance.
- **Grounding (Ancrage)**: The conscious connection to the body and the Earth.
- Axis: The inner verticality where vibrational stability resides.

This lexicon is your official reference: every term is used within the protocols of this manual.

2. Glossary of Central Concepts

Focused on feeling and information, excluding quantum terminology.

- **Grounding (Ancrage)**: The ability to stabilize one's vibrational field in the earth and matter. It is the foundation of energetic security that prevents the practitioner from being swept away by the emotions of others.

- **Vertical Axis**: An imaginary but physically felt channel, connecting the earth pole and the sky pole through the spine. It is the circulation path for the Unity of Life.
- **Energetic Sweeping**: A cleansing technique consisting of combing the vibrational field with the hands to clear away spent or polluting charges.
- **Crystallization**: Emotional or traumatic information that has densified to the point of becoming "solid" within the tissues, creating circulation blockages.
- **Frequency**: The unique signature of a vibration. Every organ, emotion, or thought possesses its own frequency (high or low, fluid or jarring).
- **Information**: The program or "DNA" carried by energy. In Vibrational Transition, information is what gives shape and quality to vital energy.
- **Tissue Reading**: The art of perceiving, through manual or intuitive feeling, the memories and charges stored in bones, muscles, and organs.
- **Modulation**: The conscious action of the mind to change vibrational frequency. This is the tool that allows one to shift from a state of stress to a state of peace.
- **Magnetic Passes**: Coded movements of the hands within the vibrational field to rebalance, soothe, or energize the consultant's flow.
- **Zero Point**: A state of absolute neutrality where the practitioner has neither expectations nor desires. It is from this point that the Vibrational Transition is most powerful.
- **Recentering**: The action of bringing all attention and energy back inside one's own body, putting an end to energetic leaks toward the outside.
- **Vibrational Transition**: The conscious process of shifting from a disordered vibrational state (suffering, fatigue, blockage) to a state of coherence and vitality.
- **Unity of Life (UV)**: A global measure of an individual's vitality and coherence. It represents the reservoir of energy available for health and consciousness.

📝 SHEET 2: Rapid Self-Recentering Protocol

Objective: Reclaim your Unity of Life and stabilize your axis in less than 60 seconds.

Usage: Before a session, after a stressful event, or whenever the mind becomes restless.

Principle: Shifting from dispersion to absolute presence through the law of the "Zero Point."

1. PREPARATION

Before acting upon the world or others, you must once again become the master of your own temple. Being "off-center" is an information leak: your particles of consciousness are scattered within your worries or within the fields of others. To recenter is to summon these particles back to sit at the heart of your cells. It is the ultimate act of sovereignty.

2. STEP-BY-STEP PROTOCOL

Step 1: The Physical Point of Support

- Action: Focus all your attention on the soles of your feet (if standing) or your sitz bones (if sitting).
- Sensation: Feel the pressure and the weight. Imagine your feet "spreading out" on the ground.
- Vibration: Energy leaves the forehead (the mind) and descends into the base.

Step 2: The Recall Breath

- Action: Take a deep breath in through the nose while slightly contracting the perineum.
- Intention: "I inhale all my scattered energies."
- Action: Exhale slowly through the mouth as if blowing through a straw, releasing the shoulders and jaw.

Step 3: Activating the Zero Point (Vibrational Heart)

- Action: Place two fingers (or your palm) on the center of the sternum.
- Visualization: Visualize a point of white light, extremely dense and fixed, inside your chest.
- Inner Decree: Say mentally: "Here and now. I am my Center."

Step 4: Aligning the Axis

- Action: Very slightly straighten the back of the neck (tuck the chin in).
- Sensation: Feel the invisible thread pulling you upward while keeping your feet heavy. This is Conscious Verticality.

3. SELF-ASSESSMENT FEELING GRID

How do you know if the recentering is effective? Check for these signals:

- **[ ] Physical**: A deep reflex exhalation (sigh) or a sudden dropping of the shoulders.

- **[ ] Vibrational**: A sensation of heat or tingling descending into the hands and legs.
- **[ ] Mental**: The flow of thoughts stops or becomes a distant, unimportant background noise.
- **[ ] Sensory**: The colors in the room appear sharper; sounds become more precise.

4. MASTER PRACTITIONER'S ADVICE

Do not try to "do" the recentering. Be the recentering. If you fight against your thoughts to stay centered, you are creating new tension. Welcome the thought, and let it pass like a cloud, simply returning to the sensation of your feet on the ground.

Practical Application: Repeat this protocol 5 times a day, even when everything is going well. This training is what will allow you, in an emergency or during a difficult session, to find your axis in a fraction of a second without even having to close your eyes.

Note of Harmonization: This sheet is the direct complement to Chapter 2.

📝 SHEET 3: Feeling Analysis Grid (Diagnostic)

The ultimate "reading" tool. It allows the practitioner to stop guessing and rely on a precise sensory map.

Objective: Accurately identify areas of blockage, leakage, or fluidity in oneself or the consultant.

Usage: During the "Reading" phase (Chapters 4 and 7), to establish an assessment before any intervention.

Principle: Translating sensations perceived by the hands or the "body-instrument" into actionable information.

1. The Art of Reading

Before seeking to "repair," the practitioner must become a "mirror." Performing a vibrational diagnosis is not about looking for a disease; it is about listening to the score the body is playing at this exact moment. Your hand does not judge; it captures a frequency. An area that "stings" or "resists" is not an enemy; it is an area calling for a Transition. Consider this grid as your alphabet: the better you know your letters, the clearer the body's messages will be.

2. The Decoding Table

Use this grid during your scan (manual or mentalized). For each area (head, plexus, organs, joints), identify the dominant sensation:

Perceived Sensation	Vibrational State	Informational Meaning	Priority Action
Intense Heat / Burning	Overload or Inflammation	Stagnant energy trying to circulate. Anger or acute stress.	**Neutralize** (Ch. 8) & Transverse passes.
Cold / Draft	Void or Leak	Depletion of the Unity of Life. Memory of shock or old sadness.	**Saturate** (Fixed imposition) & Grounding.
Density / Magnet / Resistance	Crystallization	Tissue blockage. Stored information (cellular memory).	**Tissue Reading** (Ch. 9) & 5 Elements.
Tingling / Fizzing	Active Circulation	Flow is present. Healing or awakening phase.	Accompany with **Longitudinal passes.**
Sensation of a "Hole" / Void	Rupture of the Axis	Major de-centering. The person is no longer "inhabited."	**Emergency Recentering** (Ch. 9).
Heaviness / Sticky	Vibrational Toxins	Emotional or environmental charge (pollution).	Complete **Energetic Sweeping** (Ch. 11).

3. Methodology of the Examination

1. **The Neutral State**: Complete Sheet 1 (Self-centering) before starting.
2. **Distance Scan**: Pass your hands 10 cm from the consultant's body, from head to feet.
3. **Marking**: Mentally note the 2 or 3 areas where the sensation changes radically.
4. **Validation**: Place your hand (contact or proximity) on the "densest" or "coldest" area to confirm the information.

4. Master Practitioner's Advice

Beware of "Mental Noise": The greatest risk is wanting to interpret immediately with your brain (e.g., "It's cold, so it's grief"). Stick to the pure physical sensation throughout the diagnostic. Interpretation should only come afterward to guide your choice of protocol. If you feel density, simply tell yourself: "Here, information is not flowing." This neutrality guarantees the accuracy of your Transition.

📝 SHEET 4: Step-by-Step Emotional Cleansing

Objective: Dissolve crystallizations of emotional information stored in the body (cellular memory).

Usage: Following a tissue reading that revealed an area of density, tension, or emotional "weight."

Principle: Transmutation of information through presence and breath (shifting from a solid to a fluid state).

1. Understanding Crystallization

An emotion is, by definition, energy in motion. When an emotion is not lived, expressed, or integrated, it stops. It densifies, loses its frequency of fluidity, and ends up "embedded" in the matter (fascia, organs, muscles). We then speak of an informational cyst or crystallization. Emotional cleansing is not about "analyzing" the past; it is about offering this blocked energy a vibrational exit so it can resume its journey.

2. The Operative Protocol

- **Step 1: Localization and Contact**: Place your dominant hand on the area identified during the diagnosis. Keep your hand supple. You are not massaging; you are "listening."
- **Step 2: Resonance**: Close your eyes and feel the "texture" of the blocked emotion. Is it heavy? Tight? Do not push the sensation away; dive into it. By accepting to feel it fully, you break the resistance maintaining the crystallization.
- **Step 3**: Transmutation Breath: Inhale into your own axis (Zero Point). On the exhale, direct the breath through your arm toward your hand in contact with the consultant.
- **Step 4**: Call to Fluidity: Apply the frequency of the Water Element. Visualize the tissues opening and regaining their natural elasticity.
- **Step 5**: Evacuation and Sealing: Finish with a transverse pass followed by a fixed imposition on the solar plexus to fill the space with "Peace."

3. Signs of Release

- **In the consultant**: A deep reflex sigh, yawning, liberating tears, or stomach gurgling.
- **Under the practitioner's hand**: The "hard" sensation becomes "supple." The area becomes very warm or a purifying coolness appears.

SHEET 5: Summary of Magnetic Passes

Objective: Master the gestures for directing and structuring the vibrational flow.

Usage: During treatment to move, break, or stabilize energy in the consultant's field.

1. The Philosophy of the Gesture

In Vibrational Transition, the hand is an extension of your consciousness. To perform a "pass" is to sculpt the invisible. A gesture inhabited by the intention of Transition instantly realigns disordered frequencies.

2. Technical Guide to Passes

1. **Longitudinal Passes (The Flow of Peace)**: Slow, continuous movement from head to feet. Effect: Unification of the field and soothing of the nervous system.
2. **Transverse Passes (The Charge Break)**: Sharp, shearing movement from the center outward. Effect: Disintegration of stagnant energy "cysts."
3. **Circular or Helical Passes (Dynamization)**: Small concentric circles. Clockwise to tone/fill; counter-clockwise to extract/calm. Effect: Re-launching movement.
4. **Imposition (Saturation of Presence)**: Fixed hand, open palm, 2-5 cm from the body. Effect: Deep infusion of information.

3. Variation Parameters

- **Distance: Close (2-5 cm)** for the physical/etheric body; **Distant (20-40 cm)** for the emotional body.
- **Polarity**: Dominant hand to Emit (give direction); Non-dominant hand to **Listen** (receive the echo).

4. Quick Choice Grid

If you feel...	Use the pass...	With the intention...
Stagnant heat	Transverse	"I release and evacuate"
A void or coolness	Imposition / Circular	"I nourish and awaken"
Agitation or stress	Slow Longitudinal	"I soothe and unify"
An old blockage (hard)	Tight Helical	"I drill and untie"

5. Master Practitioner's Advice

The "Light Hand": If you contract your muscles, you block your own channel. Suppleness is key. It is the intention that gives strength to the gesture, not muscular effort. Always shake your hands toward the ground after a series to release residual charges.

📝 SHEET 6: Unity of Life Tracking Chart (Logbook)

Objective: To measure, track, and stabilize your level of vibrational coherence on a daily basis.
Usage: Daily self-assessment (morning and evening) for the practitioner or the consultant.

Principle: Realizing that the Unity of Life (UV) is not a static achievement, but a flow that one learns to govern.

1. THE LOGBOOK: MIRROR OF YOUR SOVEREIGNTY

The logbook is the tool that transforms intuition into mastery. Without measurement, it is easy to drift back into old vibrational habits. By recording your state every day, you are not just logging numbers: you are dialoguing with your cells. You begin to see the correlations between your thoughts, your encounters, your diet, and your vitality. This chart is your compass to stay in the axis, even when external storms rage.

2. MEASUREMENT METHODOLOGY

The Unity of Life is measured on a scale of **0 to 100%**. It is the synthesis of four fundamental pillars. For each pillar, assign yourself a score from **0 to 25**:

- **Physical Vitality (0-25)**: Quality of sleep, absence of pain, physical strength.
- **Emotional Stability (0-25)**: Ability to remain serene, absence of impulsive reactivity, inner joy.
- **Mental Clarity (0-25)**: Capacity for concentration, absence of intrusive thoughts, presence in the moment.
- **Vibrational Feeling (0-25)**: Perception of density, heat in the hands, feeling of "connection" to the axis.

3. WEEKLY DASHBOARD (Template)

Day	Score /100 (UV)	Significant Event (Leak or Gain)	Transition Action Performed
Monday			
Tuesday			
Wednesday			
Thursday			
Friday			
Saturday			
Sunday			

4. ANALYSIS AND CORRECTION

- **UV > 80%**: State of full power. This is the ideal time for transmissions or creative projects.
- **UV 50% - 80%**: Functional but vulnerable state. Immediate recentering and grounding (Chapters 2 and 3) are recommended.
- **UV < 50%**: State of energetic survival. Stop all polluting activities. Rest, energetic sweeping, and silence are mandatory.

SHEET 7: Scripts and Invocations for Treatments

A compilation of verbal tools designed to code the treatment space and direct the **Unity of Life (UV)** with precision.

The **Word** is a tool for vibrational structuring. Words are not just sounds; they are frequencies that inform matter and the subtle bodies. Using a script or an invocation is like using a "frequential key" to open a specific door in the consultant's field.

1. Preparation Invocations (The Practitioner)

To be pronounced internally before contact to activate your High-Frequency Mind.

- **For Alignment**: "I am a pure channel between Heaven and Earth. My axis is straight, my presence is total."
- **For Neutrality**: "I leave my ego and expectations at the door. Only the Unity of Life acts through me."
- **For Active Intuition**: "I open my subtle senses. I suspend commentary to welcome raw information."

2. Opening Scripts (Setting the Framework)

To reassure the consultant's nervous system and request vibrational consent.

- **Access Request**: "With your agreement, I am now connecting to your vibrational field to identify areas of tension and restore fluidity."
- **Installing Calm**: "Allow your body to settle. With each exhale, your tissues release the old to make room for the new."

3. Transmission Invocations (During Treatment)

Direct action on blockages and intuitive reading.

- **For Dissolving a Blockage**: "Blockage information, I recognize you. Through the frequency of Unity, I release you and return you to fluidity."
- **For Expansion**: "Light and breath, circulate now in this area. May the space open, may life resume its movement."
- **The Command of the Parabola (Rapid Capture)**: "Vibrational truth, show yourself now beneath my hand."

4. Closing and Sealing Scripts (The Exit)

Marking the end of entanglement and the return to vibrational autonomy.

- **Sealing the Treatment**: "May the information from this session be sealed in your cells for your highest good. The treatment is accomplished."
- **Separation of Fields:** "I reclaim my frequency, you reclaim yours. All unnecessary links are now dissolved."
- **Return to Matter**: "Gently return to the sensation of your physical body, here and now."

5. PRACTITIONER'S ADVICE: The Vibration of Silence

The most powerful invocation is the one born from your inner silence. Let the silence allow the frequency to resonate deep within the tissues.

SUMMARY FOR YOUR PRACTICE JOURNAL

- The Word informs the energy.
- Intention directs the Word.
- Silence seals the result.

B. ENERGETIC PREPARATION EXERCISES

This is the complete and detailed version of Appendix Sheet 1. This guide is designed to be your field companion, combining the theoretical depth of the book with the technical precision of a professional training manual.

📝 SHEET 8: Grounding and Protection Before Work

It is essential to understand that the practitioner does not work alone but acts as a channel. If this channel is not solidly anchored into the ground and protected by a clear intention, it risks exhaustion or absorbing the dissonant charges from the environment. Grounding is your foundation; protection is your membrane.

1. Grounding: Connecting to Mother Earth

Grounding consists of synchronizing your frequency with that of the Earth to evacuate electromagnetic surplus and stabilize your vibrational mind.

- **The Posture**:
  - Stand with your feet parallel, hip-width apart, knees slightly unlocked to allow energy to flow.
  - Relax your shoulders and place your tongue against the roof of your mouth to close the energetic circuit.
- **Active Visualization**:
  - Imagine powerful roots growing from the soles of your feet and your base (sacrum), plunging deep into the ground.
  - With every inhale, visualize telluric energy rising into your legs.
  - With every exhale, let all your tensions, doubts, and mental noise descend into the earth.

2. Protection: Sealing the Field

Protection in Vibrational Transition is not a rigid "armor" (which would block intuition), but an expansion of your own light to create a high-frequency barrier.

- **The Light Bubble (Expansion Technique)**:
  - From your center (the heart or the Hara), visualize a sphere of white or golden light extending all around you, about one meter away.
  - **The Intention (The Word)**: Decree internally: "I am a pure channel. Only light passes through; everything lower than my frequency slides off this field."
- **Emotional Neutrality**:
  - The best protection is the "Zero Point." By remaining neutral and non-judgmental, you offer no vibrational "hook" for the consultant's energies to latch onto.

3. Flash Exercise: The Practitioner's "Ignition"

This accelerated capture and preparation exercise (derived from the Parabola technique) is performed in less than two minutes before welcoming a consultant.

1. **Instant Silence**: Close your eyes and cut off the internal commentary for 3 seconds.
2. **Activating the Hands**: Rub your palms vigorously together until you feel intense heat, then pull them 10 cm apart to feel the ball of energy.
3. **The UV Call (Unity of Life)**: Visualize a column of light passing through the crown of your head and descending into your hands.
4. **Affirmation**: "I am ready, I am a channel, I am presence."

4. Pre-Preparation Checklist

Before placing your hand on the consultant, check these four points of your vibrational sensory system:

- **Feet**: Do you feel heavy contact with the floor? (Grounding).
- **Belly**: Is your breathing low and calm? (High-Frequency Mind).
- **Heart**: Are you in an intention of neutral benevolence? (Clear-Sensing).
- **Head**: Is your mind suspended, ready to receive information? (Present Moment).

PRACTICE SUMMARY

Grounding and protection are not options; they are the very structure of your craft. A well-grounded practitioner multiplies the effectiveness of their transmission tenfold while preserving their own health capital.

📝 SHEET 9: Heart Centering and Subtle Body Alignment

It is fundamental to understand that the practitioner is not merely a technician of gesture, but a vibrational instrument. If your "antenna" (your subtle structure) is misaligned, the signal you transmit will be distorted. Heart centering is not an emotion; it is the activation of the most powerful coherence motor in the human body. Subtle body alignment ensures that your intention, emotion, and vitality are perfectly overlaid for maximum effectiveness.

1. Heart Centering: The Coherence Motor

The heart possesses its own nervous system and an electromagnetic field 5,000 times more powerful than that of the brain. By centering yourself in this space, you shift from a "noisy" mind to a high-frequency mind.

- **The Technique**:
  - Physically place one hand on the center of your chest (sternum) to focus your attention there.
  - Breathe slowly, as if the air were entering and leaving directly through your heart.
- **The Evocation**: Connect to a feeling of gratitude or neutral peace (a memory, a landscape, or simply the state of "presence").
- **The Signal**: You know you are centered when you feel a gentle warmth or a slight expansion in the chest, accompanied by immediate mental calm.

2. Subtle Body Alignment: Verticality

Your various bodies (physical, etheric, emotional, mental) can shift out of alignment due to stress or fatigue. Alignment consists of "re-nesting" them so that the Unity of Life (UL) flows without leakage.

- **The Central Axis Protocol**:
  - Visualize a vertical axis of light (the tube of light) passing through your entire body, from the crown of the head to the perineum.
  - The Feeling: Imagine your subtle bodies as discs of light. Through intention, bring all these discs back so they are perfectly centered on your vertical axis.
- **The Affirmation**: "My bodies are aligned, my axis is pure, I am unity."

3. Exercise: The Double Connection (Heaven-Earth)

This exercise merges centering and alignment to make you an operational transmission channel.

1. **Grounding**: Feel your feet and your link to the earth (see Sheet 8).
2. **Opening**: Feel the crown of your head opening toward universal energy.
3. **Junction**: Bring these two currents (rising and falling) together at the center of your heart.
4. **Radiance**: Let the energy accumulated in the heart diffuse through your arms to your fingertips.

4. Vibrational Instrument Checklist

Before starting a treatment, validate your internal state:

- **Presence**: Is my mind here, in the present moment?
- **Coherence**: Is my heart open and neutral?
- **Verticality**: Do I feel my central axis is solid and straight?
- **Availability**: Am I ready to let the energy pass through without trying to control it?

📝 SHEET 10: Opening Manual Channels and Palm Sensitization

This technical module is essential for transforming your hands into precision instruments capable of reading and transmitting subtle energy.

Understand that the hands are the direct extension of the heart and intention. If the body is the antenna, the hands are the receiving and emitting terminals. A "closed" or insensitive hand will miss crucial information in the vibrational field. Opening the manual channels fluidizes the passage of the **Unity of Life (UL)** and sharpens your **clear-sensing**.

1. Activating the Laogong Points

The center of the palm (the **Laogong point**) is the primary gateway for energetic emission. Its activation is the first step in vibrational sensory development.

- **The Technique**:
  - **Thermal Friction:** Vigorously rub your palms together for 15 to 30 seconds until you feel intense heat.
  - **Stimulating Pressure**: Using your thumb, firmly massage the center of the opposite palm with clockwise rotations.
  - **Finger Awakening**: Gently stretch each finger as if "lengthening" the meridians that terminate there.

2. Sensitization Exercise: The "Energy Ball"

This classic exercise allows you to shift from "passive perception" to "active reading" by creating immediate biofeedback (a biological phenomenon allowing the body to regulate its functions).

- **Mental Silence**: Apply the Present Moment technique by suspending all internal commentary.
- **Positioning**: Place your hands face-to-face, about 5 cm apart.
- **Compression Movement**: Very slowly move your hands a few millimeters closer and then further apart.
- **Observation**: Note the appearance of density, tingling, heat, or a magnetic resistance between your palms.
- **Expansion**: Gradually move your hands apart while trying to maintain this invisible link until the sensation fades.

3. Reading Capacity

Once the channels are open, your hands become capable of practicing the **Parabola technique** for accelerated capture. You must learn to distinguish the information received:

- **Hot**: Zone of inflammation or intense activity.
- **Cold / Empty**: Zone of devitalization or circulation blockage.
- **Tingling / Electricity**: Active circulation or nerve overload.
- **Density / Wall**: Protection or tissue resistance.

4. Vibrational Hand Checklist

Before beginning a session or intuitive reading, check your terminals:

- **Heat**: Are my palms naturally warm?
- **Fluidity**: Can I feel the energy flowing to my fingertips?
- **Neutrality**: Is my hand relaxed (without unnecessary muscle tension)?
- **Receptivity**: Am I ready to receive raw information before mental interpretation?

PRACTICE SUMMARY

Opening the hands is not a one-time act but a daily preparation. By sensitizing your palms, you move from the ordinary mind to a high-frequency mind capable of reading energy naturally.

📝 SHEET 11: Activating Intuition Before Practice

To stabilize your perceptive channel before any intervention.

It is crucial to understand that intuition is not an intellectual process, but a sensory function of your High-Frequency Mind. If you begin a session with an analytical mind ("What is wrong with them?", "Where should I put my hands?"), you saturate your channel and prevent subtle information from emerging. Activating intuition before practice means shifting from "thinking" mode to "receiving" mode.

1. The Principle: Shifting to Active Intuition

Passive intuition is spontaneous, but for the practitioner, it is necessary to master **active intuition**. This is a faculty triggered voluntarily by a change in one's internal state.

- **The Goal**: To create sufficient mental silence so that the consultant's vibrational signal is perceived without filters.
- **The Internal Stance**: Absolute emotional neutrality and directed attention, but without tension.

2. Activation Protocol

This exercise combines the **Present Moment Technique and Intuitive Expansion** to open your sensors.

- **Instant Silence (3 seconds)**:
    - Take a slow inhale and a conscious exhale to immediately lower the mental volume.
    - Suspend all internal commentary. Observe the space in front of you without naming it.
- **Opening the "Clair-Senses"**:
    - Focus your attention on your (recently activated) palms and your overall bodily feeling.
    - Decree your intention: "I am in reading mode. I receive the raw information."
- **Expansion of the Halo**:
    - Visualize your vibrational field as a halo of light extending one meter around you.
    - "Switch on the flashlight" of your field to encompass the treatment space. Feel the air density increase.

3. Flash Exercise: The Preparation Parabola

Just before placing your hand on the consultant, use this variation of the **Parabola Technique** to capture the general tone of the upcoming session:

1. **Step 1**: Visualize the question or the area to be treated.
2. **Step 2**: Launch the intention into your field like launching a probe.
3. **Step 3**: Welcome the first piece of information that returns (an image, a sensation of hot/cold, or a word).

- **Golden Rule**: Do not try to interpret. Take the first piece of information; it is the one intact from any mental filter.

4. Intuitive State Checklist

You are ready to practice when:

- **The mind is "quiet"**: Fast but silent, oriented toward reception and not control.
- **Clear-sensing is "active"**: You already perceive variations in density or temperature in the room.
- **Presence is total**: You are neither in the consultant's past nor in the future result, but in the **present moment.**

📝 SHEET 12: Harmonizing Energy Centers (Self-Balancing)

This self-balancing protocol is designed to stabilize your structure before intervening on another's, ensuring that you only transmit from a state of perfect coherence.

Harmonizing your own energy centers (or chakras) is the ultimate step in preparing the "body-instrument." A practitioner whose centers are out of sync emits a "scrambled" signal that can limit the effectiveness of the Vibrational Transition. Self-balancing ensures that your vitality, emotions, and High-Frequency Mind work in synergy.

1. The Principle: Global Coherence

The goal is not just to open the centers, but to tune them like the strings of an instrument. In training mode, we seek a fluid circulation of the **Unity of Life (UL)** from bottom to top, without areas of stagnation or overheating.

- **The Role of Centers**: Each center acts as a transformer that adapts universal energy to a specific biological or psychic function.
- **Sensory Reading**: Before balancing, use your clear-sensing to identify which center requires special attention (density, cold, or emptiness).

2. Express Self-Balancing Protocol

Use this protocol right after activating your hands to seal your alignment.

- **Grounding, Stability, Vitality – Root Chakra (Base of spine):**
  - Focus on your base. Visualize a dense **red** color. Feel the solidity of your incarnation.
- **Creation, Pleasure, Fluidity – Sacral Chakra (Lower abdomen):**
  - Breathe 3 cm below the navel. Visualize an **orange** color. Feel your vitality reservoir filling.
- **Confidence, Will, Strength – Solar Plexus Chakra (Stomach):**
  - Relax this area often tightened by stress. Visualize a radiating **yellow** sun, establishing emotional neutrality.
- **Love, Harmony, Openness – Heart Chakra (Center of chest):**
  - Activate your High-Frequency Mind by breathing into the heart. Visualize a **green** color. Allow neutral benevolence to settle in.
- **Expression, Truth, Listening – Throat Chakra:**
  - Relax the jaw to free expression. Visualize a light **blue** color.
- **Intuition, Clarity, Vision – Third Eye Chakra (Forehead):**
  - Visualize your active intuition awakening behind the forehead like an **indigo** light.
- **Spirituality, Unity, Awakening – Crown Chakra (Top of head):**
  - Open the crown for intuitive expansion. Let the UL descend as a rain of light through your central channel. Visualize a **violet/white** color.

3. Exercise: The "Figure-Eight" Circulation (The Sealing)

To harmonize the centers with each other, circulate the energy through intention.

- Imagine a flow drawing a vertical "8" connecting your heart to your base, then your heart to your crown.
- This movement creates a feedback loop that stabilizes your field and activates your vibrational mind.

4. Self-Balancing Checklist

You are harmonized when:

- **Fluidity**: You no longer feel "knots" or shadow zones in your vertical axis.
- **Temperature**: Your body is uniformly warm and vibrant.
- **Mind**: Your spirit is **clear, gentle, and silent**, ready for capture.

PRACTICE SUMMARY

Self-balancing is the guarantee of a safe and powerful practice. By aligning your centers, you shift from "effort" mode to "channel" mode, where energy flows unhindered for the greatest benefit of the consultant.

📝 SHEET 13: Purifying Your Energetic Channel

It is crucial to understand that the practitioner is a body-instrument. Just as a musician cleans their instrument to guarantee the purity of the sound, the practitioner must purify their channel so that the **Unity of Life (UL)** flows without distortion. Purification is not a mere symbolic ritual; it is a vibrational necessity to avoid "clogging" from residual charges, thought-forms, or miasmas picked up during interactions.

1. The Principle: Vibrational Transparency

The goal of this sheet is to reach a state of "**transparency**." The purer your channel, the less resistance you offer to the energy. In training mode, purification is the process of eliminating energetic "noise" that could skew your clear-sensing or exhaust your nervous system.

- **The Central Channel (Sushumna)**: This is the highway of vibrational information. If it is obstructed, transmission becomes forced and exhausting.
- **The Other's Charge**: Without regular purification, the practitioner eventually carries the densities of their consultants (stress, sadness, pain), which inevitably leads to energetic burnout.

2. Active Purification Protocol

This protocol uses the breath and directed intention to "sweep" the central channel.

- **The Breath of Fire (Rapid Cleaning):**
  - Practice brief, powerful nasal exhales while snapping the navel inward.
  - Visualize each exhale expelling dark or stagnant particles out of your field.
- **The Light Shower (Dissolution):**
  - Visualize a flow of silvery-white light entering through the crown of your head.
  - Let this light descend like a polishing liquid inside your spinal column.
  - Feel this flow carry residues down into the earth via your roots (Grounding).
- **Arm Sweeping:**
  - With your right hand, "brush" your left arm from the shoulder to the fingertips, then reverse.
  - Perform this gesture with the firm intention of detaching vibrational "glues" accumulated on your action meridians.

3. EXERCISE: The Zero Point of Purification

This exercise resets your frequency after a treatment or a heavy situation.

1. **Step 1**: Cross your arms over your chest (a gesture of protection and returning to self).

2. **Step 2**: Silently pronounce the command: "I dissolve everything that is not me. I return to my original frequency."
3. **Step 3**: Feel a shiver or a sudden lightening. This is the signal that the charge has been released.

4. Energetic Clarity Checklist

You know your channel is purified when:

- **Lightness**: You no longer feel a "weight" on your shoulders or in the plexus.
- **Mental Clarity**: Your High-Frequency Mind is clear, without intrusive thoughts related to the previous consultant.
- **Vitality**: Your energy level rises immediately after the exercise.

🗒 SHEET 14: Energetic Alignment and Centering

This exercise finalizes your preparation by sealing the unity between your physical structure and your higher faculties, guaranteeing a total and sovereign presence.

Alignment is the act of bringing all parts of your being (physical, emotional, mental) back onto a single reference axis. It is the end of "noise" and the beginning of **Verticality. Centering** consists of bringing your consciousness inside this axis, preventing any dispersion of your Unity of Life (UL) toward the outside.

1. The Principle: Coherence of the Central Pillar

The objective is to transform your system into a "**Vibrational Laser**." A laser is light where all photons are aligned and moving in the same direction. In training mode, alignment allows you to move from diffuse perception to **accelerated energetic capture.**

- High-Frequency Mind: By aligning your attention, intention, and breath, you leave the analytical mind to activate a finer, faster intelligence.
- **Presence at "Zero Point"**: This is the point of perfect balance where you are neither ahead (expecting a result) nor behind (in your memories), but in the **Present Moment.**

2. Alignment and Centering Protocol

This protocol is the final synthesis of the previous exercises. It should be performed just before the first contact with the consultant.

- **Suspension of Commentary (3 seconds)**:
    - Take a slow inhale. During the exhale, cease all internal dialogue.
    - This second of silence opens the door to your **active intuition**.
- **The Earth-Sky Axis**:
    - Feel the grounding under your feet (Sheet 8).
    - Feel the expansion at the crown of your head (Sheet 9).
    - Visualize an invisible plumb line passing through your body, aligning your pelvis, heart, and head.
- **Centering at the Hara**:
    - Bring your consciousness to your center of gravity (below the navel).
    - Feel that you are fully inhabiting the inside of your skin.

3. Exercise: Sealing the Alignment (The Parabola)

To verify your alignment, use a rapid capture test:

1. **Step 1**: Choose an object or an area in the room.
2. **Step 2**: Launch your attention toward this object, then let the information "bounce" back to your center.
3. **Step 3**: If the information (color, sensation, word) arrives instantaneously without you having to think, you are perfectly aligned.

4. Conscious Vibrational Being Checklist

Before opening the door to your consultant, validate this ultimate checklist:

- **Axis**: Do I feel "vertical" and solid?
- **Silence**: Is my mind clear, gentle, and silent?
- **Radar**: Is my vibrational sensory system in "receiving" mode?
- **Neutrality**: Am I ready to welcome what is, without wanting to change it by force?

PRACTICE SUMMARY

Alignment and centering mark the end of your energetic preparation. You are no longer a person "trying" to do a treatment; you are a **Conscious Vibrational Being** capable of reading and transforming energy naturally.

📝 SHEET 15: Energetic Sealing and Returning to the World (Ending Practice)

This final protocol is the guarantor of your long-term vibrational integrity: it marks the clear boundary between the sacred space of treatment and the return to your personal life.

It is crucial to understand that the end of a session does not stop when the consultant leaves. Without rigorous **energetic sealing**, you remain vibrationally "entangled" with the other person. Sealing is the conscious act of closing your own field and returning the responsibility of their own frequency to the consultant. This is the ultimate stage of **total vibrational autonomy**.

1. The Principle: Breaking the Entanglement

The goal is to cut the psychic and etheric bridges created during transmission. In training mode, we consider that the practitioner must "return to their own center" to avoid exhaustion through dispersion.

- Sealing the Consultant: Before they leave, you fix the treatment information into their tissues so that it does not evaporate.
- Returning to the World: This is your own re-grounding into dense matter, necessary for leaving the high-frequency mind and returning to fluid daily functioning.

2. End-of-Practice Protocol

Follow these steps as soon as physical or visual contact with the consultant is broken.

2.1. Breaking the Link (The Guillotine Gesture)

- **Action**: Bring your hands in front of your solar plexus.
- **Gesture**: Perform a sharp, crossing movement outward while exhaling loudly through the mouth.
- **Intention**: "What is yours stays with you; what is mine stays with me. The link is cut."

2.2. Informational Washing

- **Action**: Place your hands and forearms under cold running water.
- **Visualization**: The water does not just clean the skin; it carries away the residual electromagnetic charges captured by your clear-sensing.

2.3. Sealing the Aura

- **Action**: Starting from the bottom of your body, move your hands up along your central axis to the crown of your head, as if you were pulling up a zipper.
- **Effect**: This closes your field after the intuitive expansion practiced during the session.

3. Exercise: Returning to Density (Exit Grounding)

To exit the state of clear-consciousness or clear-information and return to the physical world, you must "heaviness" your frequency.

- **Step 1**: Drink a large glass of water. Water is the conductor of grounding.
- **Step 2**: Gently tap your body (arms, legs, chest) to bring consciousness back into raw physical sensation.
- **Step 3**: Walk a few steps, deliberately feeling the weight of your body on the ground.

4. Sovereign Practitioner Checklist

You have correctly ended your session if:

- **Thoughts**: Your mind is no longer "looping" around the consultant's case.
- **Body**: You feel no pain or heaviness in the areas where the consultant was suffering.
- **Space**: You have aired out the room to renew the air and the vibrational information of the space.

PRACTICE SUMMARY

Energetic sealing is the act of sovereignty that protects your health capital. By clearly separating your field from the consultant's, you allow the transition to fully integrate for them while remaining perfectly centered and available for yourself.

C. COMPLETE PROTOCOLS

A. PHYSICAL PROTOCOLS

📝 A 1. PROTOCOLE TYPE: Care Start Protocol

(Preparation, Purification, Alignment of the Energetic Channel; Activation of Intuition before Practice)

This text describes a practice of pure **Vibrational Transition**, where your body and consciousness become the sole instrument of healing.

The start is the sacred moment where the practitioner steps aside to become a pure vector for the **Unity of Life (UL)**. This protocol is not a mere technical formality; it is a frequential initiation that allows one to shift from the state of "person" to the state of "channel." This step guarantees vibrational safety and the precision of informational capture without any external tools. Your intention and feeling become the frequency.

1. OBJECTIVES AND PREPARATION

- **Objective**: Open the vibrational field, secure the session, align the practitioner and the consultant, and establish a clear reception frequency.
- **Activated Frequencies**: Centering – Grounding – Protection.
- **Position**: Seated comfortably, feet flat on the floor, spine straight but without tension.

2. THE DEPLOYED PROTOCOL (TRANSITION STEPS)

1. **Centering and Breathing Phase**
    - **Technique**: Close your eyes. Take 4 slow, conscious breaths.
    - **Vibrational Movement**: With each inhale, breathe in pure white light. With each exhale, visualize all the day's concerns dissolving into the Earth.
    - **Feeling**: Feel your weight settling, your mind calming, and your presence becoming "thicker."
2. **Purification and Channel Cleaning**
    - **Technique**: Visualize a pillar of crystalline light descending from the top of your head.
    - **Action**: This flow sweeps through your central channel (Sushumna), cleaning the walls of any stagnant or parasitic imprints.
    - **The Word (Affirmation)**: *"I purify my channel. I dissolve all interference. I am a receptacle of pure light."*
3. **Alignment and Grounding (Verticality)**
    - **Grounding**: Visualize roots of light extending from your feet and your base, plunging into the heart of the Earth. Feel this light enter your feet and rise to your heart.

- **Alignment**: Feel golden light coming from the sky, entering your Crown Chakra, and descending through the alignment of all your chakras down to the earth.
- **Feeling**: You are the living bridge between Heaven and Earth. Feel your axis become solid and vibrant: *"I am grounded to the earth, I am connected to the sky."*

4. Activation of Intuition and Perception

We leave the ordinary mind for the **High-Frequency Mind**. This is the shift from "thinking" to "capturing."

- **Suspension of Commentary**: Apply the Present Moment Technique. Cut off internal dialogue for 3 seconds.
- **The Word**: *"I activate my sensory capture. I suspend commentary to welcome the vibrational truth."*
- **Opening Clear-Information**: Focus on the palms of your hands. Feel heat or tingling rising in your palms (**Laogong Point**) and your vision broadening.
- **Vision**: Bring your consciousness to the third eye. Decree the opening of your **Clear-Information**.

5. Aura Sealing and Protection

- **Technique**: Visualize your energetic field (aura) smoothing out and densifying all around you. **Aura Scanner (Non-contact)**: At 20 cm from the body, pass your hands to identify zones of heat (inflammation/excess) or cold (void/lack).
- **The Shield**: Form a sphere of golden light impenetrable to low frequencies.
- **The Word**: *"I am protected. My aura is sealed. Only light and pure information can reach me."*

6. Entering the Consultant's Field

This is the stage of resonance—synchronizing your calm with the consultant's agitation to transmute it.

- **Initial Impulse**: Place your hand with infinite gentleness but firm intention. The treatment begins when you feel the contact with the consultant "respond" under your palm.
- **Final Intention**: *"I set aside my ego. May this treatment be realized for the highest good, in peace and harmony."*
- **Breathing**: Maintain low, slow breathing to pull the consultant's nervous system into a state of calm through the entrainment effect.

START-UP CHECKLIST

Phase	Key Action	Expected Feeling
Purification	Breath + Water	Sensation of lightness, internal "cleanliness."
Alignment	Sky/Earth Axis	Solid verticality, absence of tension.

Phase	Key Action	Expected Feeling
Intuition	Mental Silence	Sharpened sensory acuity, suspended time.
Activation	Call of the UL	Heat or tingling in the hands.

A 2. PROTOCOL: Muscular Physical Pain

(Healing through the Vibrational Transition of body and consciousness)

Physical pain is seen as a crystallization of energy where the **Unity of Life (UL)** no longer flows freely. This protocol seeks to accompany the area toward a new frequency of fluidity and regeneration.

1. OBJECTIVE AND PREPARATION

- **Objective**: Relieve tension, deeply relax tissues, and release energetic blockages.
- **Action Plans**: Physical (release), Energetic (releasing stagnation), and Conscious (return to peace).

2. THE DEPLOYED PROTOCOL

1. **Release Phase**: Breathe into the painful area, visualizing gray mist leaving the body, replaced by cool, luminous air. Affirmation: *"I release all tensions... my energy flows again."*
2. **Soothing Phase**: Imagine a cool, bluish wave reducing inflammation. **Affirmation**: *"I soothe all reactivity... my body finds balance."*
3. **Regeneration Phase**: Visualize golden light from your heart nourishing the cells of the painful area. Affirmation: *"I send deep healing to my tissues."*
4. **Restructuring Phase**: Breathe from the **Hara**, move energy to the heart, and exhale toward the treated zone to stabilize the axis.

3. SEALING AND RETURNING TO MATTER

- **Sealing**: Visualize a white/golden pillar anchoring you to the Earth.
- **Final Grounding**: Feel your weight and roots. Drink water and stretch.

A. 3 : PROTOCOL: Joint Pain

(Healing through the Vibrational Transition of Body and Consciousness)

Joints are the hinges of our movement in life. Joint pain often signals an energetic crystallization or resistance to change. This protocol aims to restore fluidity, soothe inflammation, and release cellular memories lodged in the connective tissues. In training mode, the practitioner uses no external tools: they become the vector for the frequency required to "lubricate" and clear the joint space through the sole power of intention and sensing.

1. OBJECTIVE AND PREPARATION

- **Objective**: To relieve joint pain, soothe inflammation, release crystallized blockages, and promote tissue regeneration.
- **Setting the Condition**: Enter a neutral state (Breathing, alignment, presence). Activate your high-frequency Mind through deep abdominal breathing and clear intention.

2. THE DEPLOYED PROTOCOL (TRANSITION STEPS)

1. Connection and Authorization

Before any intervention, establish the vibrational link.

- **The Word (Interior)**: "I connect to the Light of Healing Creation. I authorize this care to release inflammation and joint pain."
- **Sensing**: Feel the opening of your central channel (Intuitive expansion).

2. Cleansing Crystallizations

- **The Technique**: Use Clear-Sensing to identify areas of density or "cold" around the joint.
- **The Word**: *"Cleanse the affected area of all blocking energy."*
- **Action**: Visualize energetic debris dissolving and leaving the body through the exhale.

3. Reducing Inflammation

- **The Technique**: Send a wave of vibrational coolness (blue or silver color) directly to the core of the joint.
- **The Word**: *"Reduce inflammation in the painful areas."*
- **Sensing**: Perceive the drop in pressure and the thermal soothing within your palms.

4. Releasing Memories and Pain

- **The Technique**: Apply the Parabola exercise to capture the cellular memory associated with the pain.
- **The Word**: *"Release the pain and the associated cellular memory."*
- **Action**: Let the information surface, acknowledge it without judgment, and let it transmute into the light.

5. Restoring Mobility and Lubrication

- **The Technique**: Visualize a golden, fluid "oil of life" permeating the joint to nourish and lubricate the surfaces.
- **The Word**: *"Restore natural and fluid movement. Impregnate this field with the oil of life to nourish and lubricate."*
- **Sensing**: Feel the space expanding between the tissues.

6. Reconnecting to Vitality

- **The Word**: *"Reconnect me to my healing power and my full health."*
- **Action**: Stabilize the energy in the heart center to seal the new health frequency.

3. SEALING AND INTEGRATION

- **Sealing**: *"Stabilize the frequencies of health and relief in all dimensions of my being."*
- **Grounding**: Re-establish contact with your feet and the weight of your body on the floor.
- **Closing**: Drink plenty of water to facilitate the elimination of the released charges.

SUMMARY FOR YOUR PRACTICE

- **Frequency**: 1 to 3 times per week depending on intensity.
- **Signs of Success**: Return of flexibility, disappearance of the blocking sensation, gentle and lasting warmth.
- **Training Note:** This treatment works through **Frequency Transition**: you replace the information of "pain/stagnation" with the information of "movement/life."

📝 A. 4: PROTOCOL for Headaches / Mental Overload

(Healing through the Vibrational Transition of body and consciousness)

A headache or mental overload is a sign of localized "**hyper-frequency**." It is an accumulation of undigested informational flows creating pressure in the etheric structure of the head. This protocol acts as a pressure relief valve, allowing energy to leave the mental sphere and descend into the body.

1. OBJECTIVES AND PREPARATION

- **Objective**: Soothe headaches, release mental saturation, evacuate circular thoughts, and restore mental clarity.
- **Action Plans**: Mental (silence), Energetic (decompression), Physical (eye and cranial relaxation).
- **Phase-in**: Sit with feet flat. Close your eyes. Visualize your thoughts as an electric current progressively quieting down.

2. THE DEPLOYED PROTOCOL (TRANSITION STEPS)

1. Decompression Phase (Releasing the Overflow)

- **Technique**: Focus on your temples and forehead. Imagine the walls of your skull becoming porous.
- **Vibrational Movement**: With each exhale, visualize the pressure escaping through the crown and temples as light gray smoke.
- **The Word**: *"I release the pressure. I clear the space. I let go of everything saturating my mind."*

2. Descent Phase (Rebalancing toward the Earth)

- **Technique**: Shift your awareness from your brain to the soles of your feet.
- **Vibrational Movement**: Visualize an energetic drain from your brain, down the spine, evacuating mental surplus into the ground.
- **Sensation**: Feel your eyes relax and your jaw loosen.
- **The Word**: *"I leave the head to return to my feet. I anchor myself in the reality of the body."*

3. Cooling Phase (Thermal Soothing)

- **Technique**: Visualize a source of icy, crystalline water flowing over your forehead and eyes.
- **Sensation**: Feel the "fire" of the mind go out. The temperature of your forehead seems to drop slightly.
- **The Word**: *"I soothe the mental fire. I instill coolness and clarity into every cell of my brain."*

4. Phase of Silence and Emptiness

- **Technique**: Remain in total stillness. Welcome the void between two thoughts.
- **The Word**: *"My mind is a peaceful lake. I am in the silence of Unity."*

3. SEALING AND INTEGRATION

- **Sealing**: Visualize a protective deep-blue light enveloping your head like a soft helmet.
- **Final Action:** Drink a few sips of fresh water.
- **Affirmation**: "My thought is fluid, my vision is clear, my mind is at rest."

TRANSITION TABLE

Phase	Vibrational Shift	Desired State
1. Decompression	Compression > Expansion	Lightness in the skull.
2. Descent	Hyper-activity > Grounding	Feeling of weight in the feet.
3. Soothing	Mental Fire > Coolness	Calm eyes and relaxed jaws.

PRACTICE SUMMARY

- **Frequency**: At the first signs of tension or after an intense day of intellectual work.
- **Training Note**: Do not "analyze" the headache. Treat it simply as a volume of excess energy that needs to be moved to the ground.
- **Advice**: Gently massage your scalp during Phase 1 to help the physical body accept the vibrational transition.

📝 A. 5. PROTOCOL: Fatigue / Exhaustion / Lack of Energy / Vitality

(Healing through the Vibrational Transition of body and consciousness)

Fatigue and exhaustion are perceived as a drop in the electrical charge of the cells and a fragmentation of the energy field (leaks). This protocol aims to seal the breaches, restart the circulation of the **Unity of Life (UL)**, and reactivate the internal "battery." In training mode, the practitioner operates a frequency transition: shifting from a state of "depletion" to a state of "full charge" by using their own channel as an amplifier to awaken the consultant's dormant vitality.

1. OBJECTIVE AND PREPARATION

- **Objective**: Recharge energetic batteries, restore physical and mental vitality, seal leaks, and activate the internal life force.
- **Conditioning**: Settle comfortably with your back straight to encourage axial circulation.
- **Vibrational Intention**: *"I connect to the Light of Healing Creation. I authorize this treatment to restore my energy and deep vitality."*

2. THE DEPLOYED PROTOCOL (TRANSITION STEPS)

1. **Repair of Leaks and Blockages**
    - **Technique**: Use your Clear-sensing to scan the periphery of the aura. Identify "cold" spots or "drafts" that signal leaks.
    - **The Word**: *"I repair every crack, every leak, and every blockage in my body and energy field."*
    - **Feeling**: Visualize a mesh of golden light sealing the breaches in your envelope.
2. **Realignment of Vital Centers**
    - **Technique**: Focus successively on each chakra, from base to crown.
    - **The Word**: *"I balance my energy centers. My flow is fluid and constant."*
    - **Action**: Feel the central axis become solid and stable, like a crystal column.
3. **Deep Energetic Recharge**
    - **Technique**: Inhale through the soles of your feet, drawing from Earth's energy, and through the crown of your head, drawing from Heaven's energy.
    - **The Word**: *"I recharge myself with living, pure, and inexhaustible energy."*
    - **Feeling**: Feel a warmth or tingling reaching every cell, like a battery being filled.
4. **Activation of Cellular Vitality**
    - **Technique**: Visualize a miniature sun at the heart of every cell, lighting up intensely.

- **The Word**: *"I activate the life force in my cells and all my bodily systems. Vitality radiates within me."*
- **Action**: Exhale this force throughout your entire being to saturate your tissues with dynamism.

5. **Healing and Regeneration**
   - **The Word**: *"I receive a fortifying healing. My strengths are restored here and now."*
   - **Action**: Let the new energy stabilize in the most fatigued organs (often the adrenals).

3. SEALING AND INTEGRATION

- **Stabilization**: *"I stabilize this new energy within me. My field is full, strong, and protected."*
- **Grounding**: Feel the weight of your body and the strength flowing through your legs again.
- **Closure**: *"Thank you to the Light of Creation and to Life. All is accomplished."*
- **Physical Action**: Stretch dynamically. Drink a glass of water and, if possible, walk for a few minutes in the fresh air to lock in the vitality through movement.

TRANSITION TABLE

Phase	Vibrational Shift	Desired State
1. Repair	Dispersion > Integrity	Feeling of "gathering oneself," end of chills.
2. Recharge	Void > Fullness	Internal heat, tingling, density.
3. Activation	Atony > Vitality	Urge to move, mental clarity restored.

A. 6. PROTOCOL: Digestion / Digestive Disorders

(Healing through the Vibrational Transition of body and consciousness)

1. OBJECTIVE AND PRESENTATION

This protocol aims to rebalance the entire digestive system, release emotions crystallized in the abdominal region, and harmonize the processes of assimilation and metabolism.

2. PREPARATION: ALIGNMENT AND INTENTION

Lie down or sit quietly, hands placed on your abdomen to establish direct contact.

- **Connection**: *"I connect to the Light of Healing Creation."*
- **Authorization**: *"I authorize this treatment to release and strengthen my digestive system."*

3. PHASE 1: TOXIN CLEANSING

- **Action**: Visualize a purifying light passing through the stomach, liver, and intestines.
- **Transition**: Feel densities and blockages dissolving and draining downward.
- **Affirmation**: *"Cleanse the digestive system of toxins and blocking energies."*

4. PHASE 2: BALANCING AND METABOLISM

- **Action**: Focus on the internal rhythm of your digestive organs.
- **Transition**: Emit a frequency of balance to stabilize organic functioning and kindly activate metabolic dynamics.
- **Affirmation**: *"Balance the functioning of the digestive system. Activate my metabolism with balance and benevolence."*

5. PHASE 3: HEALING AND EMOTIONAL SOOTHING

- **Action**: Feel your abdominal space as a receptacle for emotions.
- **Transition**: Diffuse a wave of serenity to release "stuck" emotions and infuse healing energy into sensitive areas.
- **Affirmation**: *"Heal the sources of pain and imbalance. Bring peace to the emotions stuck in the abdomen."*

6. PHASE 4: RECHARGE AND STABILIZATION

- **Action**: Visualize a golden, balancing light filling your entire digestive center.
- **Transition**: Stabilize this new vibrational frequency in your physical structure.
- **Affirmation**: *"Fill the digestive center with a balancing energy. Stabilize healing and balance in the digestive system."*

7. CLOSURE AND GRATITUDE

- **Action**: Take deep breaths, feeling the lightness in your belly.

- **Thanks**: *"Thank you for the light, the healing, and the blessing received."*
- **Physical Action**: Stretch gently and drink a glass of water to facilitate physical integration.

PRACTITIONER TIPS

- **Frequency**: 2 to 3 times per week for chronic issues.
- **Synergy**: If digestive issues are stress-related, combine this with the "Stress / Anxiety" protocol.
- **Application:** This can be practiced via direct palm imposition or distance consciousness projection.

A. 7. PROTOCOL: Stomach Pain

(Healing through the Vibrational Transition of body and consciousness)

The stomach is the center of inner alchemy, where we "digest" not only food but also our emotions and experiences. Gastric pain is often a sign of emotional overload or difficulty integrating an event. This protocol aims to soothe the digestive fire, release nervous tension, and restore inner peace. The practitioner acts directly on the organ's frequency to shift from a state of contraction to a state of natural fluidity.

1. OBJECTIVES AND PREPARATION

- **Objectives**: Reduce burning sensations, soothe digestive spasms, and release suppressed emotions.
- **Conditioning**: Settle into a neutral state (Breathing, alignment, presence). Activate your **High-Frequency Mind** through clear intention and total letting go.

2. THE DEPLOYED PROTOCOL (TRANSITION STEPS)

1. **Opening Intention**

   Establish the vibrational framework of the treatment through the word.

   - **The Word**: Pronounce with conviction: *"I open this treatment to relieve and heal stomach pain."*
   - **Action**: Feel the healing energy activate within your central channel.

2. **Energetic Cleansing**

   - **Technique**: Use your Clear-sensing to identify areas of stagnation or vibrational toxicity in the gastric area.
   - **The Word**: *"I cleanse all stagnant and toxic energies related to the stomach."*
   - Feeling: Visualize dense energies leaving the body with each exhale.

3. **Release of Emotional Tensions**

   - **Technique**: Focus your attention on the link between the stomach and the nervous system.
   - **The Word**: *"I release emotional tensions and suppressed anger affecting my stomach."*
   - **Action**: Use the **Parabola** technique to identify if there is a specific emotion to be released and let it dissolve.

4. **Pain Relief and Organ Support**

   - **Technique**: Apply a wave of gentleness directly to the organ.
   - **The Word**: *"I relieve the pain. I bring energy, calm, and vibrational support to my stomach."*
   - **Feeling**: Perceive the stomach becoming "lighter" and more spacious.

5. **Harmonization and Healing**

- **Technique**: Visualize natural fluidity returning to the entire digestive system.
- **The Word**: *"My digestive system regains its harmony. Healing settles deeply into my tissues."*
- **Action**: Let the healing vibration penetrate the deep layers of the organ.

6. Balancing and Inner Peace

- **The Word**: *"I balance digestive and nervous energies. My stomach is at peace, relaxed, and light."*
- Action: Stabilize the state of global relaxation.

3. SEALING AND RETURNING TO MATTER

- **Sealing**: Seal the treatment with a frequency of divine light and harmony.
- **Grounding**: Return fully to your physical body by feeling your roots with the Earth.
- **Closure:** Thank Life. Drink a large glass of pure water to facilitate integration.

A. 8. PROTOCOLE Back Care / Back Pain

(Healing through the Vibrational Transition of body and consciousness)

The back is the pillar of our structure and the receptacle of our past burdens. Back pain often expresses an excess of responsibility or emotional memories crystallized in the spine. This protocol aims to restore fluidity to the central axis, release nervous tension, and regain inner stability.

1. OBJECTIVES AND PREPARATION

- **Objectives:** Relieve back pain (lumbar, thoracic, cervical), release crystallized memories, and realign the axis of light.
- **Conditioning:** Sit comfortably with a straight back. Take 3 deep breaths: inhale light, exhale heaviness and fatigue.
- **Opening Intention:** *"I enter the frequency of relief, alignment, and healing for my back."*

2. THE DEPLOYED PROTOCOL (TRANSITION STEPS)

1. **Cleansing Burdens and Tensions**
    - **Vibrational Movement:** Inhale, visualizing clear light rising from the base of the spine to the crown. Exhale, releasing all heaviness.
    - **Vibrational Phrase:** *"I cleanse all stagnant burdens from my back. My axis is freed and lightened."*
2. **Release of Crystallized Memories**
    - **Vibrational Movement:** Direct your breath precisely to the point of pain. Imagine the breath's vibration piercing through bone and nerve to release old information.
    - **Vibrational Phrase:** *"I release memories of pain and fatigue. I make room for fluidity."*
3. **Realignment and Flexibility**
    - **Vibrational Movement:** Visualize your vertebrae gently spacing out, creating a regenerative void. Feel the energy flow like a silk ribbon along the spinal cord.
    - **Vibrational Phrase:** *"My back regains its original flexibility. Each vertebra returns to its rightful place."*
4. **Tissue Regeneration**
    - **Vibrational Movement:** Diffuse a warm, golden light across the full width of your back. Feel the muscles relax and nourish themselves with this frequency.
    - **Vibrational Phrase:** *"Vibrational healing settles into every vertebra, every fiber, every space of my back."*

3. SEALING AND RETURNING TO MATTER

- **Final Alignment:** Visualize a line of light rising from the perineum to the crown, then descending back to the feet. Your axis is now a solid channel of balance.
- **Grounding:** Feel your back like a living tree, stable and peaceful. Say internally: *"I feel supported, stable, and at peace in my entire being."*
- **Closure:** *"The treatment is sealed in the light, for peace, strength, and harmony."*
- **Physical Action:** Stretch gently and drink a large glass of pure water.

PRACTICE SUMMARY

- **Frequency:** 1 to 3 times per week depending on the intensity of the tension.
- **Training Note:** This protocol uses **Vibrational Transition** to transform the feeling of "weight" or "blockage" into a frequency of "support" and "clarity."

A. 9. PROTOCOL: Sleep Disorders

(Healing through the Vibrational Transition of body and consciousness)

Sleep is much more than simply resting the body; it is the moment when consciousness withdraws to regenerate within the source of the Unity of Life. Sleep disorders are often a sign of a nervous system in "hyper-frequency" or a mind that refuses to let go of control. This protocol aims to soothe mental activity, harmonize circadian cycles, and induce deep peace. In training mode, the practitioner operates this transition through the calm of their own channel, drawing the consultant toward a frequency of total rest without any external tools.

1. OBJECTIVES AND PREPARATION

- **Objectives:** Soothe the nervous system, release intrusive thoughts, harmonize sleep cycles, and induce inner calm.
- **Conditioning:** Settle comfortably (preferably lying down). Practice alignment and centering (Sheet 2).
- **Opening Intention:** *"I connect to the Light of Healing Creation. I authorize the implementation of this treatment to restore and improve my sleep."*

2. THE DEPLOYED PROTOCOL (TRANSITION STEPS)

1. Cleansing Disruptive Energies

- **Technique:** Use your clear-sensing to sweep the field above the head and temples. Identify zones of electromagnetic or mental "noise."
- **The Word:** *"I cleanse all negative energy or disruptive thoughts. My mental space is freed."*
- **Action:** Visualize thoughts like clouds dissipating to reveal a pure, starry night sky.

2. Mental Soothing and Serenity

- **Technique:** Focus on the heart center and let the vibration of calm diffuse toward the brain.
- **The Word:** *"I infuse serenity and calm into my heart and mind. My system becomes peaceful."*
- **Sensation:** Feel the heart rate slow down and the pressure behind the eyes lighten.

3. Nervous System Balancing

- **Technique:** Visualize your spine as a channel of soft light. Move the energy down along the nerves to calm hyper-reactivity.
- **The Word:** *"I balance my nervous system. I shift from alert mode to rest mode."*

4. Gentle Energetic Recharge

- **Technique:** Unlike a dynamic treatment, visualize "lunar" energy here—silvery and enveloping.
- **The Word:** *"I fill myself with a gentle, balancing, and protective energy for my night."*

5. Healing of Root Causes

- **Technique:** Apply the Parabola technique to allow the subtle cause of insomnia to rise and be instantly transmuted.
- **The Word:** *"I heal the causes of insomnia and lack of rest. My body remembers how to sleep."*

6. Stabilization of Harmony

- **The Word:** *"I stabilize calm and inner peace within me. I am safe in rest."*

3. SEALING AND SURRENDER TO REST

- **Sealing:** Visualize a midnight blue protection bubble all around your vibrational field.
- **Final Action:** Stop trying to analyze. Let your consciousness slide downward, toward the earth, with total trust.
- **Closure:** *"Thank you to the Light of Creation for this rediscovered rest. All is accomplished."*

📝 A. 10. PROTOCOL: Smoking Cessation

(Healing through the Vibrational Transition of body and consciousness)

Addiction is a vibrational entanglement where an external substance fills a space of presence or anesthetizes an emotional overload. Quitting smoking through vibrational transition consists of shifting from the frequency of "need/lack" to the frequency of "freedom/fullness." The practitioner uses no substitutes: they accompany the consultant (or themselves) in cleansing the etheric imprints of tobacco and reactivating sovereign will at the heart of the cells.

1. OBJECTIVES AND PREPARATION

- **Objectives:** Release energetic imprints of tobacco, soothe nervous cravings, strengthen will, and purify the respiratory system.
- **Duration:** 35 to 45 minutes.
- **Conditioning:** Sit or lie down comfortably. Close your eyes. Place one hand on your chest, the other on your plexus.
- **Vibrational Intention:** *"I connect to the light of creation to initiate my liberation and realign with my pure essence."*

2. THE DEPLOYED PROTOCOL (TRANSITION STEPS)

1. **Presence and Dissolution of the Need**
    - **Action:** Breathe into the chest. With each exhale, feel the external need dissolve. With each inhale, feel the inner presence amplify.
    - **Sensation:** Feel a golden wave, soft and warm, settling in your thorax. This is the original frequency.
2. **Cleansing the Breath and Lungs**
    - **Technique:** Bring awareness to your throat and lungs. Spot the "gray" imprint of addiction.
    - **Movement:** Inhale pure white light. Exhale the symbolic gray smoke, dissolving into the light.
    - **Vibrational Phrase:** *"I gently cleanse all energetic imprints and memories related to this addiction. My breath is pure."*
3. **Releasing Dependency Links**
    - **Technique:** Visualize the invisible attachments between your nervous system and the smoking habit.
    - **Movement:** By the power of your intention, "sever" these threads of dependency.
    - **Vibrational Phrase:** *"I detach from what is not me. I reclaim my sovereignty."*
4. **Activation of Sovereign Will**
    - **Technique:** Focus on your solar plexus (the center of will).

- **Movement:** Visualize an inner sun growing, burning away the last impulses of craving.
- **Vibrational Phrase:** *"My will is aligned with my light. I choose freedom and life."*

5. **Forgiveness and Compassion**

- **Phrase:** *"I forgive myself and welcome myself with love. I choose to respect myself totally."*

3. SEALING AND RETURNING TO MATTER

- **Final Sealing:** *"I integrate this liberation into all my cells and all my planes of existence."* Feel the original creation vibration unite with your new frequency. You are free.
- **Grounding:** Hands on heart and belly. Thank your body and consciousness.
- **Closure:** *"I seal this treatment in peace, strength, and light. All is accomplished."*
- **Physical Action:** Drink water slowly. Walk a little and observe the calm that has settled in.

TRANSITION TABLE

Step	Vibrational Shift	Desired State
1	Dependency > Presence	Connection to the source
2	Poison > Purity	Cleansing of the breath
3	Attachment > Detachment	Release of links
4	Weakness > Mastery	Activation of the will
5	Conditioning > Freedom	Reconnection to essence

PRACTICE SUMMARY

- **Frequency:** Withdrawal phase: every day for 7 days, then space out according to feeling.
- **Advice:** Hydrate often. Each time a craving arises, breathe consciously to transform the reflex into presence.
- **Note:** This treatment works by substituting the "frequency of lack" with the "frequency of the whole being."

A. 11. PROTOCOL: Addictions – Drugs

(Healing through the Vibrational Transition of body and consciousness)

Addiction to heavy substances is perceived as a profound fragmentation of inner unity, where invasive frequencies saturate the reward circuits and the etheric field. This protocol works through vibrational transmutation: the conscious shift from a frequency of dependency and lack to a frequency of freedom, clarity, and reconnection to the Essence. The practitioner acts directly on the body's informational circuits to reprogram balance patterns without any external tools.

1. OBJECTIVES AND PREPARATION

- **Objectives:** Release vibrational imprints of dependency, purify the energy field, restore willpower, and reconnect consciousness to inner freedom.
- **Conditioning:** Settle into a quiet space. Sit or lie down with a straight back and relaxed shoulders.
- **Vibrational Intention:** *"I now free myself from all forms of dependency and reclaim my inner freedom, my health, and my alignment."*

2. THE DEPLOYED PROTOCOL (TRANSITION STEPS)

1. **Connection to the Creative Light**
    - **Action:** Visualize a soft golden light descending from the top of your energy field, entering through the crown of your head.
    - **Sensation:** Feel this frequency diffuse into your brain, immediately soothing nervous agitation.
2. **Cleansing and Purification**
    - **Technique:** Identify areas of "grayness" or density in your aura, often around the head and the liver.
    - **Vibrational Movement:** Visualize this golden light acting as a solvent that dissolves impurities.
    - **Vibrational Phrase:** *"I cleanse my body and mind of all toxic imprints. I purify my blood, my cells, and my subtle bodies."*
3. **Release of Memories of Lack**
    - **Technique:** Breathe deeply into your solar plexus. With each exhale, let go of the sensation of emptiness or anxiety.
    - **Vibrational Phrase:** *"I release the memories of lack and suffering. I choose fullness here and now."*
4. **Breaking Energetic Links of Addiction**
    - **Technique:** Visualize the invisible threads connecting you to the substance as discordant frequencies.
    - **Action:** Through a decree of your consciousness, "sever" these links.

- **Vibrational Phrase:** *"I cut all vibrational links with the drug and former circles of influence. I reclaim my power."*

5. **Restoration of Strength and Will**

- **Technique:** Bring your attention to your belly (the Hara). Feel a blue flame of protection and strength ignite there.
- **Vibrational Phrase:** *"I regain my inner strength. My will is pure, solid, and sovereign."*

6. **Deactivation of Altered Reward Patterns**

- **Technique:** Visualize your neural circuits realigning to a frequency of natural satisfaction and peace.
- **Vibrational Phrase:** *"I free my brain from false pleasure circuits. I open myself to the real joy of being."*

7. **Programming a New Reality**

- **Vibrational Phrase:** *"I create within me new patterns of balance, respect, and consciousness."*
- **Sensation:** Feel the vibrational transition taking place within your cellular structure.

8. **Global Energetic Rebalancing**

- **Action:** Imagine a golden wave rising from feet to head, re-harmonizing each chakra.
- **Vibrational Phrase:** *"I integrate perfect balance into all my dimensions. I am in harmony."*

9. **Inner Healing and Integration**

- **Action:** Feel your heart radiate and diffuse its light throughout your body, which has become conscious light.
- **Vibrational Phrase:** *"I heal my deep wounds. I regain my inner peace. I integrate the light of creation into all my cells."*

3. SEALING AND RETURNING TO MATTER

- **Sealing:** Stabilize the energy with three deep breaths.
- **Grounding:** Feel your feet in contact with the ground. Drink water mindfully to anchor the frequency into matter.
- **Closure:** Thank Life, your body, and your consciousness. All is accomplished.

PRACTICE SUMMARY

- **Frequency:** 7 consecutive days during the critical phase, then whenever the urge or tension reappears.

A. 12. PROTOCOL: Weight Loss

(Healing through the Vibrational Transition of body and consciousness)

Body weight is often a crystallized reflection of emotional protection, ancient memories, or a metabolism that has become desynchronized from the **Unity of Life (UL)**. This protocol does not aim for forced weight loss, but rather a Vibrational Transition toward a "healthy weight" by shifting from the frequency of "retention/storage" to the frequency of "fluidity/balance." The practitioner acts upon the regulation centers (hunger, satiety, metabolism) through the sole power of intention and informational sensation.

1. OBJECTIVES AND PREPARATION

- **Objective:** Harmonize frequencies related to weight, digestion, and food-related emotions. Promote natural weight loss by releasing metabolic memories and blockages.
- **Conditioning:** Settle comfortably, either sitting or lying down. Practice three deep breaths to expand your breath into the belly and solar plexus.
- **Vibrational Intention:** *"I open a vibrational process of transformation to reclaim a balanced weight, a harmonious metabolism, and a peaceful relationship with my body."*

2. THE DEPLOYED PROTOCOL (TRANSITION STEPS)

2.1. Liberation Phase (Dissolving the Old)

- **Emotional Release:** Focus your attention on your solar plexus. Breathe into this area and decree: *"I release the emotions, protections, and useless weights that I carry."* Feel the area become lighter.
- **Metabolic Cleansing:** Visualize your cells evacuating toxins and stagnant fats. *"I cleanse my body of everything that hinders my natural balance."*

2.2. Regulation Phase (Harmonizing the Present)

- **Adjustment of Hunger and Satiety:** Bring your awareness to your stomach and your nervous system.
- **Vibrational Movement:** Visualize an internal adjustment knob aligning itself with the frequency of "just satiety."
- **The Word:** *"I install the frequency of satiety, balance, and motivation. I listen only to the real needs of my body."*
- **Metabolism Activation:** Feel a gentle heat circulating through your entire system to stimulate the transformation of energies.

2.3. Self-Love and Acceptance Phase (Grounding)

- **Technique:** Visualize your body enveloped in a pink or golden light.
- **The Word:** *"I honor my body as it is today. I love it, I respect it, and I support it in its transformation."*
- **Sensation:** Feel every cell illuminate with this vibration of balance.

3. SEALING AND INTEGRATION

- **Integration Light:** Focus above your head. A white light descends, passes through your entire body, and radiates at 360°.
- **Final Sealing:** *"I integrate this frequency into all my cells, for my highest good. I am in harmony with my body, my food, and my life."*
- **Grounding:** Feel your feet and your pelvis; reconnect with physical matter.
- **Closure:** Thank your body and the light. Drink a large glass of water mindfully to anchor the change.

TRANSITION TABLE

Phase	**Vibrational Shift**	**Desired State**
1. Liberation	Retention > Evacuation	Immediate sensation of lightness.
2. Regulation	Compulsion > Satiety	Inner calm and mental clarity.
3. Integration	Judgment > Self-Love	Unity and harmony with the body.

PRACTICE SUMMARY

- **Frequency:** Repeat this treatment 3 to 7 times within the month to consolidate the new metabolic frequency.
- **Training Note:** This protocol uses Vibrational Transition to reprogram the psyche/body relationship. Success lies in maintaining the "Self-Love" frequency between sessions.
- **Recommendation:** Eat in a state of calm and presence, breathing between each bite to honor the vibrational work performed.

📝 A. 13. PROTOCOL: Strengthening the Immune System

(Healing through the Vibrational Transition of body and consciousness)

The immune system is perceived as the intelligent shield of the **Unity of Life (UL)**. It is not just about "fighting" the outside world, but about maintaining a strong and integral vibrational identity. This protocol aims to densify the aura, stimulate the defense organs (thymus, spleen, bone marrow), and raise the overall frequency to make the terrain inhospitable to low vibrations. The practitioner operates this strengthening through the luminous "tensioning" of the cells, without any external tools.

1. OBJECTIVES AND PREPARATION

- **Objectives:** Intensify natural defenses, purify the energy field of vibrational intruders, and restore global vitality.
- **Precautions:** This care acts on the energetic level and complements a healthy lifestyle.
- **Conditioning:** Seated or lying position, hands on the solar plexus or chest. Slow, deep breathing.
- **Starting Intention:** *"I connect to the divine light to initiate the treatment and strengthen my natural defenses. I intensify the energy and protection of my body."*

2. THE DEPLOYED PROTOCOL (TRANSITION STEPS)

1. **Vibrational Opening and Cleansing**
    - **Technique:** Visualize a sweep of white light starting from the center of the body toward the outside.
    - **Action:** Identify areas of fatigue or "breaches" in your energy.
    - **The Word:** *"I cleanse my vibrational field of any disruptive influence. My terrain is pure and sovereign."*
2. **Activation of the Defense Shield**
    - **Technique:** Focus your attention on the **Thymus** (center of the chest, above the heart).
3. **Vitality and Inner Strength**
    - **Technique:** Visualize a golden-red light at the base of your spine (bone marrow) rising toward the heart.
    - **Sensation:** Feel the density of your physical presence increase. You feel "full" and solid.
    - **The Word:** *"I receive deep vitality. My blood and my cells carry the frequency of perfect health."*
4. **Harmonization of Systems**

- **Technique:** Imagine a wave of peace crossing through all your organs.
- **The Word:** *"I balance my biological systems. Everything within me collaborates for my full health."*

3. SEALING, GROUNDING, AND LIGHT

- **Gratitude:** *"I thank my body and the energy for this strengthening."*
- **Grounding:** *"I fix this energy and strengthening in my body and my consciousness."*
- **Final Sealing:** *"The treatment is sealed in the Light to support my health and protection. All is accomplished."*

4. DAILY EXPRESS SELF-CARE (5-7 min)

- One hand on the heart, the other on the plexus.
- Visualize energy circulating in a loop between your two hands.
- Affirm: *"My immune system is strong, my body is protected, my light is my shield."*

📝 A. 14. PROTOCOL: Vibrational Detox of the Physical Body

(Healing through the Vibrational Transition of body and consciousness)

Detoxification is not just a biochemical process; it is a purification of the information stored in the water of our cells. The physical body accumulates material toxins, but also vibrational residues (stress, waves, memories). This protocol aims to fluidify the body's natural filters and release heavy loads.

1. OBJECTIVES AND PREPARATION

- **Objectives:** Purify filtering organs (liver, kidneys, lungs, skin), release informational toxins, and restore cellular vitality.
- **Conditioning:** Settle comfortably. Practice Earth-Heaven alignment.
- **Vibrational Intention:** *"I open this treatment to purify my physical temple. I release everything that hinders my clarity and original health."*

2. THE DEPLOYED PROTOCOL (TRANSITION STEPS)

1. Phase of Cleansing and Opening

- **Technique:** Focus your attention on your entire skin, your largest detox organ.
- **Vibrational Movement:** Visualize your pores opening and releasing dark or dense vapor.
- **The Word:** *"I cleanse my body of all impurities, toxins, and stagnant memories."*

2. Drainage of Filtering Organs (The Elimination Triangle)

- **The Liver:** Focus under the ribs on the right. Feel an emerald green light that fluidifies and cleanses.

3. Cellular Transmutation (The Silver Shower)

- **Technique:** Visualize a very fluid silver light flowing inside your blood and lymphatic vessels.
- **Sensation:** Feel the movement of an internal "deep cleaning." Perceive a sensation of lightness spreading through your limbs.
- **The Word:** *"Every cell of my body rejects density and regains its original transparency."*

4. Reset and Clarity

- **Technique:** Once the cleansing is felt, saturate the empty space with a sparkling white light.
- **The Word:** *"I install the frequency of purity and new vitality. My body is clear, my mind is free."*

3. SEALING AND RETURNING TO MATTER

- **Final Sealing:** *"I integrate this purification into all my structures. The treatment is sealed in the Light."*
- **Grounding:** Feel your feet, move your hands gently. Return fully to the sensation of a "new" body.
- **Physical Action: Drink a large glass of lemon water or pure water immediately** to physically support the detox process.

TRANSITION TABLE

Phase	**Vibrational Shift**	**Desired State**
1. Opening	Saturation > Release	Sensation of heat or chills.
2. Drainage	Stagnation > Flow	Sensation of internal movement.
3. Clarity	Opacity > Transparency	Great mental clarity and physical lightness.

PRACTICE SUMMARY

- **Frequency:** Ideal during seasonal changes or after a period of fatigue/excess.
- **Training Note:** This protocol is particularly effective if the practitioner maintains a frequency of "absolute neutrality." Do not seek to "push" toxins; let the frequency of purity dissolve the density.

B. EMOTIONAL PROTOCOLS

B. 15. PROTOCOL: Releasing Stress, Anxiety, and Nervous Tension

(Healing through the Vibrational Transition of body and consciousness)

Stress and anxiety are frequencies of "contraction" and "acceleration" that disconnect the being from its natural rhythm. This protocol aims to soothe the mind, relax the nervous system, and restore a state of deep serenity. The practitioner operates via **Vibrational Transition**: guiding the shift from a frequency of survival (stress) to a frequency of life (peace) using only presence, breath, and directed intention.

1. OBJECTIVE AND PREPARATION

- **Objective:** Soothe the mind, relax the nervous system, dissolve accumulated stress, and restore deep inner serenity.
- **Conditioning:** Sit comfortably or lie down. Close your eyes. Feel the contact of the ground or surface beneath you. Bring your awareness into your physical body.
- **Vibrational Intention:** *"I enter into a vibrational transition toward a state of calm, peace, and inner balance. I allow my energy to retune to the frequency of serenity."*

2. THE DEPLOYED PROTOCOL (TRANSITION STEPS)

1. **Release of Charges (Dissolution of Stress)**
    - **Technique:** Focus on the area of your body where you feel the most tension: neck, plexus, stomach, head...
    - **Vibrational Movement:** Inhale deeply a golden light. Exhale, imagining stress flowing out of you like gray smoke dissolving into the light.
    - **The Word:** *"I free myself from stress, fears, and emotional overload. My nervous system relaxes, my breathing calms."*
    - **Sensation:** Perceive an immediate lightening, a warmth, or a shiver of release.
2. **Repair and Coherence**
    - **Technique:** Focus your attention on your heart and your central nervous system (spine).
    - **The Word:** *"I repair the effects of stress on my body and mind. Every cell rediscovers its coherence, strength, and intelligence."*
    - **Sensation:** Feel a denser vibration or a fine heat circulating—a sign of re-harmonization.
3. **Diffusion of Healing**

- **Technique:** Visualize your body filled with emerald-green light.
- **Vibrational Movement:** Feel this light move through your entire being, repairing, soothing, and balancing.
- **The Word:** *"I receive the soothing and regenerative vibration of healing. My body, my heart, and my mind realign in harmony."*

4. Grounding Peace

- **Technique:** Visualize a column of white light descending from the Heavens through you into the Earth.
- **The Word:** *"I now anchor peace, serenity, and balance in all my dimensions. I am aligned, stable, and in harmony with Life."*
- **Sensation:** Your energy field densifies; your presence strengthens.

3. SEALING AND RETURN TO PEACE

- **Gratitude:** *"I thank the Light, Life, and all the forces of Love that accompanied me in this treatment. I choose to remain in inner peace, here and now."*
- **Final Action:** Remain still for a few moments. Slowly return to your surroundings.
- **Closure:** Drink a large glass of water to integrate the new frequency into matter.

TRANSITION TABLE

Phase	Vibrational Shift	Desired State
1. Release	Contraction > Relaxation	Fuller breathing, end of tensions.
2. Repair	Disorder > Coherence	Mental calm, sense of unity.
3. Grounding	Instability > Serenity	Feeling of security and solidity.

PRACTICE SUMMARY

- **Frequency:** Practice as soon as the need arises, or daily during periods of high tension.
- **Training Note:** The success of this protocol lies in the **exhale**: it is the breath that carries the transition from the "stress" frequency to the "peace" frequency.

📝 B. 16. PROTOCOL: Emotional Blockages, Grief, and Shock

(Healing through the Vibrational Transition of body and consciousness)

A shock or grief creates an informational "crystallization" that freezes energy in the past. The body keeps the imprint of pain as an impassable zone of density. This protocol aims to fluidify these areas, release undigested emotions, and restore the being's radiance.

1. OBJECTIVES AND PREPARATION

- **Objectives:** Release old or recent emotional blockages, soothe memories of shock or grief, cleanse heavy charges (sadness, anger, despair), and restore inner peace.
- **Conditioning:** Settle in a quiet place. Close your eyes. Take three deep breaths, sending the breath down into the pelvis.
- **Vibrational Intention:** *"I connect to the Source to initiate this emotional release treatment. My intention is to release the charges related to this shock (or grief) to rediscover my full light."*

2. THE DEPLOYED PROTOCOL (TRANSITION STEPS)

1. **Cleansing and Opening**
    - **Technique:** Scan your body to locate the emotional "lump" or "knot" (often in the heart or plexus).
    - **The Word:** *"I cleanse my vibrational field of all dross and densities related to this ordeal."*
    - **Action:** Imagine a water of light flowing through this area to dissolve the crystallization.
2. **Release of Trauma**
    - **Technique:** Focus on the center of the shock. Do not flee the sensation; breathe through it.
    - **The Word:** *"I release the imprint of trauma from my cells. I release the pain, the shock, and the dread."*
    - **Sensation:** Feel the area relax, like a hand letting go.
3. **Alchemy of Emotions**
    - **Technique:** Welcome the dominant emotion (sadness, anger, emptiness) without judgment.
    - **The Word:** *"I transform my pain into peace. I let my emotions flow so they may return to the Source."*
    - **Action:** Visualize these emotions as a river finally flowing freely.
4. **Frequency of Forgiveness and Reconciliation**

- **The Word:** *"I grant myself forgiveness. I release guilt and judgment. I make peace with what was."*

5. **Restoration of Serenity**

- **The Word:** *"I install inner peace and gentleness in every corner of my being. My heart grows still."*
- **Sensation:** A sensation of cotton or gentle warmth envelopes your chest.

6. **Recharge and Realignment**

- **The Word:** *"I recharge myself with a new and living energy. I balance my physical, energetic, and emotional bodies."*

3. SEALING AND INTEGRATION IN THE LIGHT

- **Sealing:** *"I integrate this treatment into the Light of Creation. My being is now aligned, freed, and at peace."*
- **Grounding:** Feel your feet sink into the ground. Return to the here and now, feeling lighter.
- **Closure:** *"All is accomplished. Thank you."*
- **Physical Action:** It is common to feel the need to cry or sleep after this treatment. Welcome this natural process. Drink plenty of water.

TRANSITION TABLE

Phase	Vibrational Shift	Desired State
1. Liberation	Shock/Loyalty to pain > Release	Deep breathing, liberating tears.
2. Alchemy	Sadness/Anger > Acceptance	Sense of fluidity, end of compression.
3. Peace	Emptiness/Despair > Fullness	Warmth at the heart, soothing.

PRACTICE SUMMARY

- **Frequency:** Practice as soon as a shock occurs, or weekly during a grieving process.
- **Training Note:** In **Vibrational Transition**, the key is **acceptance**. The more you fight the emotion, the more it crystallizes. By accepting it fully, it changes frequency on its own.

B. 17. PROTOCOL: General Emotional Harmonization

(Healing through the Vibrational Transition of body and consciousness)

Emotional balance is the key to vibrational health: our emotions are moving frequencies which, when stagnant, create distortions in our field. This protocol aims to fluidify the flow of emotional currents, stabilize moods, and restore a resonance of peace. The practitioner operates through **Vibrational Transition**: they do not seek to suppress the emotion, but to tune it to the frequency of the **Unity of Life (UL)** so that it regains its function as a harmonious messenger.

1. OBJECTIVES AND PREPARATION

- **Objectives:** Balance emotional variations, soothe inner storms, release residues of daily stress, and restore vibrational stability.
- **Conditioning:** Settle comfortably with your back supported. Place one hand on the heart center and the other on the solar plexus.
- **Vibrational Intention:** *"I harmonize my emotional world. I choose to move from agitation to clarity, and from contraction to expansion."*

2. THE DEPLOYED PROTOCOL (TRANSITION STEPS)

1. **Scanning and Fluidity**
    - **Technique:** Identify areas of "knots" or "weight" in your chest and abdomen.
    - **Vibrational Movement:** Visualize a wave of luminous water circulating from top to bottom, carrying away emotional residues.
    - **The Word:** *"I cleanse and I release all stagnant emotions. I let energy flow freely within me."*
2. **Soothing the Solar Plexus**
    - **Technique:** Concentrate your breath in the area between your navel and your sternum (the seat of emotions).
3. **Heart-Consciousness Alignment**
    - **Technique:** Connect your heart (pure emotion) to your head center (consciousness) through feeling.
    - **Vibrational Movement:** Visualize a bridge of pink and white light between these two centers.
    - **The Word:** *"I balance my feelings and my thoughts. I am centered in the intelligence of the heart."*
4. **Integration of Gentleness**
    - **Technique:** Envelop your entire energy field in a frequency of compassion and gentleness.

- **The Word:** *"I welcome myself with gentleness. I am at peace with what I feel."*

5. Stabilization Finale

- **Technique:** Saturate your aura with a sparkling white light that stabilizes the new frequencies.
- **The Word:** *"I stabilize harmony within me. My emotional structure is clear and luminous."*

3. SEALING AND RETURN TO BALANCE

- **Grounding:** Feel your pelvis and your legs as solid. Emotional balance requires strong rooting.
- **Closure:** *"The treatment is sealed in peace. I am in harmony with myself and with the world. All is accomplished."*
- **Physical Action:** Take three deep breaths while smiling slightly. Drink water to fix the information.

TRANSITION TABLE

Phase	Vibrational Shift	Desired State
1. Cleansing	Clutter > Fluidity	Sensation of "unburdening," lightness.
2. Harmonization	Storm > Dead Calm	Calm and regular abdominal breathing.
3. Stabilization	Fragility > Solidity	Feeling of inner security.

📝 B. 18. PROTOCOL: Releasing Limiting Beliefs

(Dissolving limiting beliefs that hinder evolution and reinstalling positive, aligned beliefs)

A limiting belief is an energetic "label" stuck onto our reality, acting as a filter that reduces our field of possibilities. This protocol aims to dissolve these fixed mental structures to replace them with frequencies of expansion and truth.

1. OBJECTIVES AND PREPARATION

- **Objectives:** Dissolve restrictive thought patterns, release unconscious locks that hinder evolution, and reinstall positive beliefs aligned with the Essence.
- **Conditioning:** Settle comfortably. Close your eyes. Breathe consciously to center yourself in your inner space.
- **Vibrational Intention:** *"I release all my limiting beliefs and I install positive beliefs aligned with my deep truth."*

2. THE DEPLOYED PROTOCOL (TRANSITION STEPS)

1. **Identification of the Belief**
    - **Technique:** Focus on your mind and your heart. Ask yourself: *"Which belief is holding me back today?"*
    - **Sensation:** Identify the feeling of contraction associated with this thought. Locate it in your body.
    - **Vibrational Movement:** Recognize this frequency as simple information that you are about to transform.
2. **Bringing the Limitation to Light**
    - **Technique:** Bring your consciousness to the crown of your head.
    - **Action:** Visualize the "limit" as a zone of density or a veil obscuring your vision.
    - **Vibrational Phrase:** *"I identify this limitation and I decide to step out of it here and now."*
3. **Dissolution and Liberation**
    - **Technique:** Use your breath as an energetic broom over your head and plexus.
    - **Vibrational Movement:** With each exhale, feel the structure of the belief disintegrating and leaving your field.
    - **The Word:** *"I release this belief from my cells, from my mind, and from my DNA. I detach from it totally."*
4. **Installation of Truth**
    - **Technique:** Focus your attention on your heart and solar plexus.
    - **Vibrational Movement:** Let a pure and stable light emerge at the center of your being. This is your original truth.

- **The Word:** *"I install my truth. I manifest who I truly am, beyond conditioning."*
- **Sensation:** Feel an immediate expansion in the chest.

5. **Grounding the Realization**

- **Technique:** Diffuse this new frequency of "possibility" throughout your body, down to your feet.
- **The Word:** *"I anchor my new reality. I am free to create my life according to my highest vibration."*

3. SEALING AND INTEGRATION

- **Final Sealing:** *"I am free from all my limiting beliefs. I manifest my truth in matter. All is accomplished."*
- **Grounding:** Feel your body solid, your feet grounded. Take a deep breath of victory.
- **Physical Action:** Write down the new positive affirmation that replaces the old belief in your notebook. Drink water to fix the information.

TRANSITION TABLE

Phase	**Vibrational Shift**	**Desired State**
1. Identification	Ignorance > Clarity	Awareness of the blockage.
2. Liberation	Contraction > Space	Sensation of lightening in the head.
3. Installation	Lie > Truth	Sensation of power at the plexus.
4. Realization	Doubt > Certainty	Feeling of capability and freedom.

PRACTICE SUMMARY

- **Frequency:** Practice as soon as a thought of "I can't" or "I don't deserve" appears.
- **Training Note:** In **Vibrational Transition**, the belief is not fought; it is dissolved by the introduction of a higher frequency (Truth).
- **Advice:** Pay attention to synchronicities in the following days: they are signs that your vibrational field has shifted its frequency of realization.

B. 19. PROTOCOL: Releasing Emotional Shock

(Releasing the imprints of recent or ancient trauma and emotional shock)

An emotional shock is a shockwave that "freezes" space-time inside the body. Whether recent or ancient, it creates a distortion in the vibrational field that continues to emit a frequency of fear or pain. This protocol aims to release these traumatic imprints to restore the original fluidity of the being. The practitioner operates via **Vibrational Transition**: guiding consciousness into the storage areas of the shock to dissolve its structure through the power of intention and light alone.

1. OBJECTIVES AND PREPARATION

- **Objectives:** Release traumatic imprints and emotional shocks, evacuate the informational charge linked to the event, and restore auric protection.
- **Conditioning:** Settle in a quiet place. Adopt slow, deep breathing to center yourself.
- **Vibrational Intention:** *"I release all my emotional shocks from this life and other lives, here and now. I authorize my being to transmute these memories into peace."*

2. THE DEPLOYED PROTOCOL (TRANSITION STEPS)

1. Identification of the Shock

- **Technique:** Focus your attention on your forehead (mind) and your solar plexus (seat of the shock).
- **Sensation:** Identify the feeling of "freezing," coldness, or emptiness associated with the trauma.
- **The Word:** *"I bring the imprint of the shock to light. I recognize this frequency without letting it overwhelm me."*

2. Release of the Associated Emotion

- **Technique:** Move your consciousness toward your sacral chakra (lower abdomen) and your heart.
- **Vibrational Movement:** Visualize the blocked emotion (fear, shock, sadness) as a wave starting to become liquid again.
- **The Word:** *"I let the emotion flow and evacuate. It no longer defines me; it leaves my sacred space."*

3. Dissolution and Liberation

- **Technique:** Shift your attention to all body areas that still feel "tight" or affected by the memory.
- **Vibrational Movement:** With each exhale, feel the trauma structure disintegrating and leaving your field like light dust.
- **The Word:** *"I dissolve the roots of the shock in all my dimensions. I am free."*

4. Healing and Restoration

- **Technique:** Flood your entire body and aura with a soft, restorative, and soothing light.
- **Sensation:** Feel the energetic "holes" or "tears" caused by the shock closing up.
- **The Word:** *"I receive deep healing. My vibrational field regains its integrity and strength."*

5. Sealing and Protection

- **Technique:** Visualize a membrane of protective light all around your aura, about 50 cm from your body.
- **The Word:** *"I seal my space. I am safe. My light is my shield."*

3. SEALING AND INTEGRATION

- **Closure:** *"I am free from all past shock. My vibration is clear, my heart is at peace. All is accomplished."*
- **Grounding:** Feel your feet, reconnect with physical matter.
- **Physical Action:** Drink water mindfully and allow yourself a time of rest to permit full integration of the new frequency.

TRANSITION TABLE

Phase	**Vibrational Shift**	**Desired State**
1. Identification	Forgetfulness/Denial > Clarity	Awareness of the shock's location.
2. Liberation	Freezing > Flow	Sensation of movement or internal heat.
3. Healing	Pain > Soothing	Sense of relief and wholeness.
4. Protection	Vulnerability > Strength	Sensation of solidity and security.

B. 20. PROTOCOL: Healing Repetitive Patterns

(Healing and transmuting negative or limiting repetitive patterns)

A repetitive pattern is a frequency loop that feeds itself in the unconscious, constantly bringing us back to the same limiting situations or reactions. This protocol aims to break these closed circuits to open the being to new timelines.

1. OBJECTIVES AND PREPARATION

- **Objective:** Heal and transmute negative or limiting repetitive patterns, release self-sabotage mechanisms, and restore freedom of choice.
- **Conditioning:** Settle in a quiet place. Breathe deeply to align your body and mind.
- **Vibrational Intention:** *"I heal my negative repetitive patterns. I release the loops of the past to embrace my full sovereignty."*

2. THE DEPLOYED PROTOCOL (TRANSITION STEPS)

1. **Identification of the Pattern**
    - **Technique:** Focus on your forehead (mind) and the back of your neck (unconscious memory).
    - **Sensation:** Feel the pattern's structure, often perceived as a gear or a repetition of circular thoughts.
    - **The Word:** *"I bring the repetitive pattern to light. I identify the loop that keeps me in the past."*
2. **Detection of the Repetition**
    - **Technique:** Move your consciousness toward your solar plexus and belly (seat of habits).
    - **Vibrational Movement:** Identify the resonance of that which "constantly returns."
    - **The Word:** *"I recognize the frequency of repetition. I decide to stop this movement today."*
3. **Healing and Transmutation**
    - **Technique:** Visualize a healing light crossing through your entire physical and etheric body.
    - **Vibrational Movement:** Feel the energetic fibers of the pattern relaxing and transforming.
    - **The Word:** *"I send healing to the heart of my system. I transmute the limit into expansion."*
    - **Sensation:** A feeling of heat or untying in the previously identified zones.
4. **Release of the Loop**

- **Technique:** Expand your consciousness to your aura (all around you).
- **Vibrational Movement:** Imagine that the closed circles surrounding you open to become ascending spirals.
- **The Word:** *"I free myself from attachment to my old patterns. I step out of the loop."*

5. Sealing by Light

- **Technique:** Flood your entire being with a sparkling white light.
- **The Word:** *"I seal this transformation in the Light. My path is clear, my future is new."*

3. SEALING AND INTEGRATION

- **Closure:** *"My repetitive patterns are healed and transmuted. I walk toward my new reality. All is accomplished."*
- **Grounding:** Feel your body as new, vibrate with the joy of liberation. Reconnect with your feet on the ground.
- **Physical Action:** Drink pure water. Be attentive to changes in reactions or thoughts in the coming days.

TRANSITION TABLE

Phase	Vibrational Shift	Desired State
1. Identification	Automatism > Awareness	The "click," seeing the trap.
2. Transmutation	Crystallization > Fluidity	Physical release, end of oppression.
3. Liberation	Confinement > Opening	Sensation of fresh air, mental clarity.
4. Sealing	Instability > Solidity	Feeling of strength and determination.

PRACTICE SUMMARY

- **Frequency:** Practice as soon as you spot a situation that "looks like" a past failure.
- **Training Note:** In **Vibrational Transition**, we do not seek to understand the psychological "why," but to modify the "energetic signature" that attracts the pattern.
- **Advice:** This treatment gains power if followed by a concrete action that differs from your usual habits.

B. 21. PROTOCOL: Reconnection / Awakening of Joy and Serenity

(Healing through the Vibrational Transition of body and consciousness)

Joy is not a fleeting emotion but the natural state of the **Unity of Life (UL)**. Ordeals and stress create veils of grayness that hide this frequency. This protocol aims to dissolve existential heaviness and nostalgia to allow the light of the heart to emerge once more. The practitioner operates via **Vibrational Transition**: guiding the shift from a frequency of "heavy survival" to a frequency of "light living" by reactivating the soul's resonance within every cell.

1. OBJECTIVES AND PREPARATION

- **Objectives:** Rediscover lightness and inner peace, dissolve blockages to joy, release existential tensions, and reconnect to the vibration of the soul.
- **Conditioning:** Settle into a comfortable space. Connect to your inner light and the peace of the heart.
- **Vibrational Intention:** *"My intention is to dissolve inner heaviness and reactivate the simple joy of being alive. I connect to the peace of my heart."*

2. THE DEPLOYED PROTOCOL (TRANSITION STEPS)

1. **Cleansing of the Aura and Channels**
    - **Technique:** Focus your attention on the energy field all around you.
    - **Vibrational Movement:** Visualize a rain of golden light cleansing away all dust of sadness and fatigue.
    - **The Word:** *"I cleanse my vibrational field of all negativity. I make room for clarity."*
2. **Releasing Inner Limits**
    - **Technique:** Identify areas of contraction in your body (often the throat or plexus).
    - **Vibrational Movement:** Exhale slowly, feeling the inner barriers dissipate.
    - **The Word:** *"I free myself from my emotional blockages and my limitations. I open myself to the infinite."*
3. **Dissolution of Sadness**
    - **Technique:** Bring your consciousness deep into your heart.
    - **Sensation:** Welcome any nostalgia or "vague à l'âme" (soul-weariness), then imagine an inner sun evaporating this mist.
    - **The Word:** *"I remove sadness from my heart. I let melancholy be transformed into luminous wisdom."*
4. **Healing and Opening of the Heart**

- **Technique:** Place your hands on your sternum. Feel the warmth of your touch.
- **Vibrational Movement:** Breathe in the frequency of Universal Love. Feel your heart radiating at 360°.
- **The Word:** *"I repair my heart in light and gentleness. I choose to live in love and openness."*

5. Awakening of Joy and Serenity

- **Technique:** Form a slight smile. Feel this vibration sparkling in your belly and rising toward your face.
- **Sensation:** Connect to the vibration of pure gratitude—without an object, just the joy of being here.
- **The Word:** *"I rediscover my natural zest for life. I am filled with a deep and lasting serenity."*

3. SEALING AND GRATITUDE

- **Gratitude:** *"I cultivate thankfulness for this moment of grace. Thank you to Life."*
- **Sealing (Gold):** Visualize a crystalline white light sealing this treatment into all your cells.
- **Closure:** *"All is accomplished. I am joy, I am peace."*
- **Physical Action:** Stretch as if waking from a long sleep. Drink a glass of water and carry this inner smile throughout your day.

TRANSITION TABLE

Phase	Vibrational Shift	Desired State
1. Cleansing	Opacity > Clarity	Sensation of vibrational cleanliness, lightness.
2. Heart Alchemy	Sadness > Peace	Warmth in the chest, free breathing.
3. Awakening	Gravity > Sparkling	Urge to smile, "champagne bubble" sensation.
4. Integration	Fleeting > Stable	Feeling of wholeness and security.

PRACTICE SUMMARY

- **Frequency:** Practice as soon as a feeling of heaviness sets in, or every morning to inform your day with the frequency of joy.
- **Training Note:** In **Vibrational Transition**, joy is not something we look for outside; it is what remains once the veils have been removed (cleansing).
- **Advice:** The activation of gratitude (Phase 3) is the most powerful engine of this treatment. Find three small details in your life to say "Thank you" for during the process.

C. ENERGY PROTOCOLS

📝 C. 22. PROTOCOL: Chakra + Aura + Meridian Realignment

This protocol is the very architecture of vibrational health. It involves bringing the three pillars of subtle anatomy back into phase: the centers (**Chakras**), the envelopes (**Aura**), and the circuits (**Meridians**). The practitioner operates through **Vibrational Transition**: every pendulum rotation becomes an inner wave, every label becomes a state of consciousness, and every Hebrew vibration becomes a frequency to be embodied through sensation.

1. PREPARATION AND CONNECTION

- **Objective:** Establish the light channel and ground oneself in the Source.
- **Position:** Sitting or standing, spine straight, hands on the heart and belly.
- **Technique:** Breathe three times. Visualize a thread of light descending from the Heavens to your crown and another rising from the Earth to your tailbone.
- **The Word (Connection):** *"I connect to the Divine Light and to the pure Source of Creation."*

2. THE DEPLOYED PROTOCOL (TRANSITION STEPS)

1. **Cleansing of the Aura and Envelopes**
    - **Technique:** Place your hands a few centimeters from your body. Feel the thickness of your energy field.
    - **Vibrational Movement:** Perform a slow sweep with your hands (or through your consciousness alone) from top to bottom, all around you.
    - **The Word:** *"I cleanse my aura of all stagnant energy, all parasitic thoughts, and everything that is not aligned with my original light."*
    - **Sensation:** Feel the air become lighter around you.
2. **Alignment and Harmonization of the Chakras**
    - **Technique:** Bring your attention successively to the 7 major centers, from the base to the crown.
    - **Vibrational Movement:** At each center, imagine a wheel of light balancing itself, centering, and radiating its pure color.
    - **The Word:** *"I align and balance my chakras. May each center vibrate at its perfect frequency, in harmony with all others."*
3. **Fluidification of the Meridians**
    - **Technique:** Feel the lines of force running through your arms, legs, and torso.

- **Vibrational Movement:** Visualize currents of golden light circulating at high speed in these channels, dissolving blockages.
- **The Word:** *"I release the circulation of energy in all my meridians. My vitality is fluid, constant, and unhindered."*

4. **Repairing Energy Leaks**

- **Technique:** Scan your auric envelope. If you feel a zone of "cold" or "emptiness," direct your breath toward it.
- **The Word:** *"I repair and seal every breach in my vibrational field. My aura is whole, strong, and protective."*

5. **Sealing in the Light**

- **Technique:** Visualize a sparkling white light condensing all around your aura, forming a soft and stable shield.
- **The Word:** *"I seal this realignment in the Divine Light. I am protected, balanced, and centered."*

3. CLOSURE AND GRATITUDE

- **Gratitude:** *"I thank the Divine Light and the Source of Creation for the care, healing, and balancing received today. Amen."*
- **Final Sealing:** *"I seal and close all unwanted openings and connections in the Divine Light and under Its protection."*
- **Physical Action:** Drink a large glass of pure water. Breathe deeply three times, feeling your feet and pelvis in contact with the ground.

RECAP TABLE

Dimension	Vibrational Shift	State of Consciousness
AURA	Clutter > Clarity	Expansion of the field outward.
CHAKRAS	Misalignment > Axis	Perfect verticality and internal stability.
MERIDIANS	Stagnation > Flow	Sensation of tingling and heat.

📝 C. 23. PROTOCOL: Complete Body-Soul-Spirit Harmonization

(Uniting and harmonizing the physical, energetic, emotional, mental, and spiritual planes in unity)

The human being is perceived as a multidimensional unit where body, soul, and spirit must vibrate in unison to manifest health and realization. This protocol aims to reunite and harmonize all planes within unity. The practitioner operates through **Vibrational Transition**: they no longer separate the planes but realign them on a single frequency of coherence—that of the **Unity of Life (UL)**.

1. OBJECTIVE AND PREPARATION

- **Objective:** Reunite and harmonize all planes of the being in perfect unity.
- **Conditioning:** Deep breathing and complete recentering. Settle into a flexible verticality, whether sitting or standing.
- **Vibrational Intention:** *"I harmonize my body, my soul, and my spirit in perfect unity."* (Or if on another: *"I harmonize the body, soul, and spirit of [Name] in perfect unity."*)

2. THE DEPLOYED PROTOCOL (TRANSITION STEPS)

1. **Harmonization of the Physical Plane**
    - **Technique:** Focus on your entire physical shell, from the soles of your feet to the top of your skull.
    - **Vibrational Movement:** Breathe into every organ, muscle, and bone. Feel the density of your body become luminous and vibrant.
    - **The Word:** *"I harmonize my physical body. I bless the temple of my presence on Earth."*
2. **Alignment of the Soul**
    - **Technique:** Focus your consciousness on the heart chakra and the center of the head.
    - **Vibrational Movement:** Feel the subtle link uniting your deep desires, your emotions, and your eternal essence. Visualize pink and blue light intertwining in the center of your chest.
    - **The Word:** *"I harmonize my soul. I align with my life path and my sacred mission."*
3. **Awakening of the Spirit**
    - **Technique:** Move your consciousness to the upper part of your body, your neck, and the space just above your head.
    - **Vibrational Movement:** Feel the opening to the field of pure consciousness, where thought becomes creation. Visualize a column of sparkling white light.

- **The Word:** *"I harmonize my spirit. My consciousness is clear, connected, and radiant."*

4. **Fusion in Total Harmony**
   - **Technique:** Perform circular consciousness movements (or use your hands in your auric field) encompassing your entire body.
   - **Vibrational Movement:** Feel the point of fusion where the body, soul, and spirit form a single harmonic note.
   - **The Word:** *"I install perfect harmony in all my dimensions. I am a being of unity."*
5. **Sealing in the Light**
   - **Technique:** Visualize yourself at the center of an impenetrable golden sphere of light.
   - **The Word:** *"I seal this unity in the Light. I am complete, I am one, I am peace."*

3. INTEGRATION AND CLOSURE

- **Validation Test:** Breathe and ask yourself: *"Am I ready to embody this harmony today?"* Feel the "Yes" vibrate in your belly.
- **Grounding:** Feel the weight of your harmonized body on the ground. It is in matter that this unity must express itself.
- **Closure:** *"All is accomplished. Thank you to the Source, thank you to Life."*

SUMMARY TABLE

Phase	**Plan of Transition**	**Vibrational Result**
1. Body (Physical)	Matter > Vibration	Sensation of presence, heat, life.
2. Soul	Emotion > Essence	Inner peace, sense of belonging.
3. Spirit	Mind > Consciousness	Clarity, high vision, connection to the All.
4. Harmony	Separation > Unity	Sense of wholeness and quiet strength.

PRACTICE ADVICE

- **Frequency:** This treatment is the "great retuning." Ideally practiced once a week or during major life changes.
- **Training Note:** In **Vibrational Transition**, the importance is not to mentally understand each plane, but to feel that you occupy the entire space of your being, with no shadow zones.

📝 C. 24. PROTOCOL: Comprehensive Chakra Care

Chakras are the entry and exit points for vital energy. Their balance (opening, closing, fluidity) determines our overall state of health. This protocol aims to diagnose and harmonize each of the 7 main centers. The practitioner operates through **Vibrational Transition**: they replace the pendulum with their own sensory perception and use focused intention to transmute blockages directly in the body, without external tools.

1. PREPARATION AND PROTECTION OF THE PRACTITIONER

- **Objective:** To become a pure and secure channel.
- **Conditioning:** Settle in a quiet place. Take 3 deep breaths to ground yourself (Heaven-Earth connection).
- **The Mudra of Universal Intelligence:** Place your hands in a triangle shape in front of your heart.
- **Call to the Source:** *"Source of the Universe, please raise my energy."* Feel the frequency shift within you.
- **Intention:** *"I open myself to be a pure channel of healing. I am protected from all low-frequency energies. Only energies of light and love may pass through me."*

2. THE DEPLOYED PROTOCOL (DIAGNOSIS AND HARMONIZATION)

- **Vibrational Evaluation:** Focus your attention on each center. Instead of a pendulum, feel in your hand or your own body if the area is: *Hot/Cold, Fluid/Tight, Radiant/Lethargic.*
- **Inner Question:** *"Is this chakra balanced?"* Listen to the response of your felt sense.
- **Harmonization of the 7 Major Centers:** For each chakra, bring your awareness to the area, breathe into it, and use the associated word:
    - **ROOT Chakra (Base of spine):** *"I anchor my presence and my security. I am stable."*
    - **SACRAL Chakra (Lower belly):** *"I release my creativity and my emotions. I am fluid."*
    - **SOLAR PLEXUS Chakra (Stomach):** *"I radiate my personal power in peace. I am solar."*
    - **HEART Chakra (Center of chest):** *"I open my heart to unconditional love. I am love."*
    - **THROAT Chakra (Throat):** *"I express my truth with rightness. I communicate."*
    - **THIRD EYE Chakra (Forehead):** *"I open my inner vision. I see with clarity."*

- **CROWN Chakra (Top of head):** *"I connect to the universal consciousness. I am One."*

3. GLOBAL HARMONIZATION AND SEALING

- **General Cleansing:** Sweep your consciousness from head to toe, then across the front and back of the body. *"I harmonize and cleanse my entire system. May fluidity be restored in all my centers."*
- **Final Sealing:** Visualize a golden or white light "sealing" each chakra in its state of perfect balance. *"I seal this treatment in the light. My system is balanced, protected, and radiant."*

TRANSITION TABLE

Center	Detected State	Vibrational Shift
Lower (1-2-3)	Contraction / Fear	Grounding > Quiet Strength
Median (4)	Closure / Weight	Isolation > Heart Opening
Upper (5-6-7)	Fog / Agitation	Confusion > Spiritual Clarity

📝 C. 25. PROTOCOL: Purification of Family Karma

(Purifying karmic memories and family lineages that hinder evolution, health, or abundance)

Family karma is perceived as a web of invisible memories and obligations transmitted through lineages. This protocol aims to purify these memories to free both the individual and their ancestors. The practitioner uses breath, intention, and feeling to alchemize inherited densities.

1. PREPARATION AND CONNECTION

- **Objective:** Establish the bridge between self, light, and lineage.
- **Technique:** Eyes closed. Three deep breaths. Inhale light through the crown, exhale any weight or legacy of density.
- **Call of Presences:** Hand on heart, other on the belly (root). *"I call upon the presence of my Higher Self, and I invite the ancestors of light to accompany me."*
- **Visualization:** See a column of golden light enveloping you and feel your lineage unfolding behind you.

2. THE DEPLOYED PROTOCOL (TRANSITION STEPS)

1. **Identifying Karma:** Focus simultaneously on the solar plexus and root chakra. Feel patterns or weights that do not belong to you. *"I bring to light the karmic memories of my lineage that hinder my evolution."*
2. **Family Reconciliation:** Focus on the heart. Send a wave of compassion toward all who preceded you. *"I honor my lineage. I bring peace and reconciliation to my family's history."*
3. **Purification of Memories:** Visualize a rain of white light passing through every layer of your family tree. *"I purify the memories of pain, lack, and fear inherited from my ancestors."*
4. **Release of Bonds:** Feel the invisible links to the past. Imagine these bonds untying to become threads of free light. *"I free myself and I free my lineage. We are now free to move forward in the light."*
5. **Illumination and Unification:** Visualize divine light crossing the entire lineage. *"Divine light passes through my lineage and lights my path. All is now at peace, purified, and unified."*

3. SEALING AND INTEGRATION

- **Final Affirmation:** *"My family karma is purified. I release my lineage and move forward free in the light of my destiny. All is accomplished."*
- **Physical Action:** Drink pure water. If emotions arise in the following days, welcome them as necessary waves of purification.

TRANSITION TABLE

Phase	**Inner Movement**	**Vibrational Effect**
1. Karma	Plexus/Root grounding	Revelation of lineage patterns.
2. Family	Heart opening	Reconciliation and compassion.
3. Purification	Descending white breath	Deep cleansing of memories.
4. Liberation	Release of tensions	Reclaimed sovereignty.

C. 26. PROTOCOL: Rebalancing Polarities (Yin/Yang)

(Healing through the Vibrational Transition of body and consciousness)

The balance between the **Feminine (Yin)** and the **Masculine (Yang)** is the foundation of creative harmony. An imbalance can manifest as a difficulty in taking action (excess Yin) or a difficulty in feeling and resting (excess Yang). This protocol aims to harmonize these two forces for right grounding and action. In training mode, the practitioner operates through **Vibrational Transition**: using the geography of their own body (left and right) to feel and unify these two currents in the central axis, without external tools.

1. OBJECTIVES AND PREPARATION

- **Objective**: Balance feminine and masculine polarities for harmonious grounding and action.
- **Conditioning**: Stand or sit with a straight back. Close your eyes. Become aware of the separation between the left and right halves of your body.
- **Vibrational Intention**: *"I perfectly balance my feminine and masculine energies. I unite receiving and giving within the unity of my being."*

2. THE DEPLOYED PROTOCOL (TRANSITION STEPS)

1. **Activation of the Yin Polarity**
    - **Technique**: Focus exclusively on the left side of your body (reception, intuition, feminine).
    - **Vibrational Movement**: Breathe as if air enters only through your left nostril and descends throughout your left side. Feel the softness and depth.
    - **The Word**: *"I honor and activate my Yin polarity. I open myself to intuition, receptivity, and inner calm."*
2. **Activation of the Yang Polarity**
    - **Technique**: Shift your attention to the right side of your body (action, structure, masculine).
    - **Vibrational Movement**: Feel the strength, heat, and uprightness of this side. Breathe as if air circulates in every muscle on the right side.
    - **The Word**: *"I honor and activate my Yang polarity. I strengthen my capacity for action, my clarity, and my structure."*
3. **Harmonization and Fusion**
    - **Technique**: Bring your awareness to the central axis (the spine).
    - **Vibrational Movement**: Visualize the two currents (left and right) meeting and intertwining along your spine, like two spirals of light.
    - **The Word**: *"I harmonize my two polarities. They unite to create perfect balance at the center of my being."*

4. Global Alignment

- **Technique**: Feel this union diffusing from the central axis to your entire body and aura.
- **The Word**: *"I align my thought, my feeling, and my action. I am unified in all my dimensions."*
- **Sensation**: A sense of wholeness; no longer feeling "divided" or "leaning" to one side.

5. Sealing and Protection

- **Technique**: Visualize a balancing light (often perceived as pearly white or soft blue) surrounding your body.
- **The Word**: *"I seal this balance and protect my vibrational field. I remain centered and serene."*

3. SEALING AND INTEGRATION

- **Gratitude**: *"Thank you to the sacred balance within me."*
- **Closure**: Take a deep breath and feel your two hands naturally join together in front of your heart (a gesture of unity).
- **Physical Action**: Drink a glass of water to fix this balance in matter. Walk a few steps to feel the new stability of your stance.

TRANSITION TABLE

Phase	Body Side	Vibrational Shift
1. To Do	Left	Passivity > Conscious Receptivity
2. This One	Right	Brute force > Right Action
3. Balance	Center	Duality > Unity
4. Alignment	Whole Body	Blur > Perfect Alignment

PRACTICE SUMMARY

- **Frequency**: Practice whenever you feel indecisive or, conversely, too controlling.
- **Training Note**: In **Vibrational Transition**, Yin/Yang balance is a sensation of "equal weight" between left and right. If you feel one side is "emptier" than the other, send more breath there.

C. 27. PROTOCOL: Subconscious Cleansing

(Healing through the Vibrational Transition of body and consciousness)

(Releasing memories, fears, programming, and limiting beliefs in the subconscious)

The subconscious is like a hard drive where our memories, fears, and beliefs have been stored since conception. This data dictates our automatic reactions. This protocol aims to clear these cumbersome archives to reclaim our sovereignty. The practitioner uses their consciousness as a beam of light to identify, clean, and reprogram mental storage zones (crown, frontal, occipital).

1. OBJECTIVE AND PREPARATION

- **Objective:** Release memories, fears, and limiting programs anchored in the subconscious.
- **Conditioning:** Settle into absolute silence. Adopt deep, slow breathing. Feel your mind quiet down and your body settle.
- **Vibrational Intention:** *"I cleanse my subconscious and release all limiting memories, beliefs, and programs. I open the space for my original truth."*

2. THE DEPLOYED PROTOCOL (TRANSITION STEPS)

1. Connection to the Subconscious

- **Technique:** Focus on three key areas of your head: the top (**Crown**), the forehead (**Frontal**), and the back of the skull (**Occipital**).
- **Vibrational Movement:** Feel the vibration of these areas. If you feel pressure, density, or tingling, this is where information is ready to be processed.
- **The Word:** *"I access my subconscious with clarity and safety. I bring to light what must be released."*

2. Cleansing Phase

- **Technique:** Focus your awareness on the entire cranium and the back of the neck.
- **Vibrational Movement:** Visualize a stream of crystalline water or a breeze of light passing through your brain, carrying away debris and old images.
- **The Word:** *"I cleanse all negative memories and obsolete programs. My mind becomes crystal clear."*

3. Cellular Release

- **Technique:** Feel the information descend from the head to the rest of your body.
- **Vibrational Movement:** With each exhale, feel your cells letting go of fears and tensions linked to the past.

- **The Word:** *"I release my body and spirit from any grip of the past. I am free."*
- **Sensation:** A sense of global lightening, as if a weight has left your shoulders.

4. **Conscious Reprogramming**
   - **Technique:** Focus simultaneously on your head (consciousness) and your heart (integration).
   - **Vibrational Movement:** Install a new frequency of peace, confidence, or joy. Imagine writing new lines of light in your mind.
   - **The Word:** *"I reprogram my subconscious with thoughts of love, success, and peace. My new reality is taking hold now."*

5. **Sealing and Protection**
   - **Technique:** Visualize a protective blue light surrounding your aura.
   - **The Word:** *"I protect my subconscious. My vibrational field is sealed in the light."*

3. SEALING AND INTEGRATION

- **Validation Test:** Ask yourself: *"Are there still memories to clean today?"* The feeling should be calm and neutral.
- **Closure:** *"My subconscious is purified and harmonized. All is accomplished."*
- **Physical Action:** Drink a large glass of water to facilitate the evacuation of released charges. Remain in silence for a few minutes to stabilize the new frequency.

SUMMARY TABLE

Phase	Transition Zone	Desired State
1. Connection	Head (Top/Front/Back)	Access to archives, tingling.
2. Cleansing	Brain / Neck	Mental clarity, cool sensation.
3. Liberation	Whole body	Total letting go, lightening.
4. Reprogramming	Head / Heart	Sense of renewal and possibility.

PRACTICE ADVICE

- **Frequency:** This protocol is powerful. Practice it in the evening before sleep to allow integration to occur overnight.
- **Note:** Pay attention to your dreams within 48 hours; they are often signs of the final subconscious evacuation.

C. 28. PROTOCOL: Aura Cleansing

(Healing through the Vibrational Transition of body and consciousness)

The aura is the shield and mirror of our inner state. It can accumulate "larvae" (energy parasites), energetic debris, or present leaks and negative charges following difficult interactions or shocks. This protocol aims to restore the integrity and purity of this field. In training mode, the practitioner operates through **Vibrational Transition**: using etheric tactile sensitivity and intention to sweep, repair, and seal their light envelope without any external tools.

1. OBJECTIVES AND PREPARATION

- **Objective:** Remove energy parasites, debris, leaks, and negative charges from the auric field to regain clarity and protection.
- **Conditioning:** Create your sacred space through silence and presence. Drink a glass of water to promote energetic conductivity.
- **Vibrational Intention:** *"I cleanse and purify my aura of all non-aligned energy. I restore my luminous integrity here and now."*

2. THE DEPLOYED PROTOCOL (TRANSITION STEPS)

1. **Cleansing and Purification Phase**
    - **Technique:** Place your hands about 20-30 cm away from your physical body.
    - **Vibrational Movement:** Perform slow, circular movements all around you, as if "combing" your aura. Sense areas of density, cold, or tingling.
    - **The Word:** *"I cleanse my aura. I cut the ties (Hitukh Keshrim) and I dissolve the debris that does not belong to me."*
    - **Sensation:** A feeling of increasing fluidity in the space surrounding your body.
2. **Auric Repair**
    - **Technique:** Focus your attention on the areas where you felt "holes" or weaknesses during the previous step.
    - **Vibrational Movement:** Use your breath and the positioning of your hands (without touching the body) to "smooth" and close these breaches. Visualize a web of light weaving itself to plug the leaks.
    - **The Word:** *"I repair my energetic envelope. I close every leak and strengthen the structure of my shield of light."*
3. **Sealing and Protection**
    - **Technique:** Visualize a sparkling golden or white light condensing at the periphery of your aura.

- **Vibrational Movement:** Feel this light becoming a semi-permeable membrane: it lets out excess energy but allows only love and light to enter.
- **The Word:** *"I seal my protection. My aura is strong, pure, and impenetrable to dissonant frequencies."*

3. SEALING AND INTEGRATION

- **Validation Test:** Ask internally: "Does my aura still require cleaning today?" Observe if the feeling around you is now homogeneous and vibrant.
- **Closure:** *"My aura is clean, repaired, and protected. I give thanks for this care. All is accomplished."*
- **Physical Action:** Drink pure water again. Take a deep breath while opening your arms as if to embrace your own energy field.

SUMMARY TABLE

Phase	Vibrational Action	Desired Result
1. Cleansing	Slow circular sweeping	Evacuation of heavy and parasitic charges.
2. Repair	Focus on "voids"	End of energy leaks, sense of solidity.
3. Protection	Peripheral densification	Stable radiance and inner security.

📝 C. 29. PROTOCOL: Activation of the 12 DNA Strands (Layers)

(Healing through the Vibrational Transition of body and consciousness)

DNA is not just a biological structure but a multidimensional library containing our spiritual potentials, our galactic heritage, and our connection to the Divine. This protocol is a journey through the 12 sacred layers of DNA. In training mode, the practitioner operates through **Vibrational Transition**: using their own cellular structure as an antenna, activating each frequency through specific gestures and precise intentions (The Word).

1. PREPARATION AND OPENING THE PORTAL

- **Objective:** Prepare the physical and energetic vessel for high frequency.
- **Posture & Mudra:** Place your hands in a triangle shape in front of your heart (Mudra of Universal Intelligence).
- **Breathing:** Breathe deeply 3 times. Feel the opening of the inner portal.
- **Vibrational Intention:** *"I activate and harmonize the 12 sacred layers of my DNA, for my perfect alignment, optimal health, and full radiance in universal love."*

2. THE DEPLOYED PROTOCOL (ACTIVATION STEPS)

1. **Field Purification (Preparatory Phase)**
    - **Gesture:** Move your hands slowly down in front of your body as if removing dense veils.
    - **The Word:** *"I purify all my energy fields."*
    - **Sensation:** A sense of clearing and immediate lightness.
2. **Activation of Biological and Terrestrial Layers**
    - **Gesture:** Place your hands on your lower abdomen, then on your solar plexus.
    - **The Word:** *"I activate my biological vitality, my terrestrial heritage, and my divine identity. My physical body aligns with original perfection."*
3. **Awakening the Layers of Wisdom and Creation**
    - **Gesture:** Place your hands on your heart and throat.
    - **The Word:** *"I activate the wisdom of the inner master and my creative power. I communicate my truth with love."*
4. **Integration of Galactic and Karmic Wisdom**
    - **Gesture:** Place your hands on your temples, then behind the neck.
    - **The Word:** *"I purify my karmic memories and activate my connection to higher dimensions. My consciousness expands."*

5. Illumination of Divine Layers

- **Gesture:** Raise your hands high above your head, palms to the sky.
- **The Word:** *"I open my divine potential. I unite with the Source and my ultimate essence. I illuminate myself with spiritual light."*

6. Cosmic and Cellular Integration (Fusion)

- **Gesture:** Bring your hands down very slowly from the sky to your heart.
- **Sensation:** Imagine the energy descending: *Cosmic > DNA > Cells > Physical Body.*
- **The Word:** *"I perfectly integrate all these activations into every cell of my body."*

3. SEALING AND STABILIZATION

- **Grounding:** Place your hands flat on your thighs. Feel the energy stabilizing in your pelvis and feet.
- **Closure:** *"All is accomplished. I am activated, aligned, and radiant. Thank you."*
- **Physical Action:** Drink a large glass of pure water to help your cells integrate the new information. Take a moment of rest or walk in nature.

SUMMARY TABLE

Grouping	Vibrational Focus	Transition State
Layers 1 to 3	Matter & Survival	Toward Divine Vitality.
Layers 4 to 6	Expression & Heart	Toward Master Identity.
Layers 7 to 9	Karma & Universe	Toward Liberation and Expansion.
Layers 10 to 12	Divinity & Unity	Toward Fusion with the Source.

PRACTICE ADVICE

- **Note:** In **Vibrational Transition**, DNA reacts to the "Frequency of Feeling." Don't just try to visualize helices; try to feel every cell in your body beginning to glow like a tiny star.

📝 C. 30. PROTOCOL: Transgenerational Cleansing

(Healing through the Vibrational Transition of body and consciousness)

Transgenerational cleansing addresses the charges, unspoken secrets, and burdens inherited from our ancestors that stagnate within our energetic structure. This protocol aims to release these memories for oneself and for the entire lineage. The practitioner operates through **Vibrational Transition**: using the visualization of the family tree and bodily resonance to dissolve the knots of the past and restore fluidity to the family heritage, without external tools.

1. OBJECTIVE AND PREPARATION

- **Objective:** Release memories and heavy charges stemming from family lineages (paternal and maternal).
- **Conditioning:** Settle into your sacred space. Breathe deeply to align your body and mind.
- **Vibrational Intention:** *"I release heavy transgenerational memories for myself and my lineages. I choose clarity and peace for my heritage."*

2. THE DEPLOYED PROTOCOL (TRANSITION STEPS)

1. **Connection and Transgenerational Cleansing**
    - **Technique:** Focus your attention on your entire body, from head to toe.
    - **Vibrational Movement:** Visualize your family tree lighting up all around you. Imagine a wave of light traveling through every branch of this tree.
    - **The Word:** *"I cleanse the memories of my ancestors. I illuminate every branch of my family tree with the light of consciousness."*
2. **Release of Charges**
    - **Technique:** Identify sensations of weight or tightness in your body (often in the back or chest).
    - **Vibrational Movement:** With each exhale, feel these heavy memories detaching and dissolving into space.
    - **The Word:** *"I release and dissolve the burdens, secrets, and debts that do not belong to me. I return to the earth what must be transformed."*
3. **Repair and Harmonization**
    - **Technique:** Bring your consciousness to your heart and diffuse a healing light toward your roots.
    - **Vibrational Movement:** Feel the energy becoming fluid again between you and your ancestors. Visualize the energetic "knots" of the tree untying.

- **The Word:** *"I repair wounded bonds. I bring harmony and forgiveness to my entire family structure."*

4. Protection and Integrity

- **Technique:** Visualize a protective light surrounding your entire aura, healthily separating you from past influences.
- **The Word:** *"I protect my vibrational field. I keep the love of my ancestors and I let go of their suffering."*

3. SEALING AND CLOSURE

- **Validation Test:** Ask internally: *"Is this cleansing accomplished today?"* Feel the response in the lightness of your body.
- **Closure:** Thank your lineages for the life passed down and thank the Source for the liberation achieved.
- **Physical Action:** Drink a large glass of pure water to facilitate the cellular integration of this new freedom.

RECAP TABLE

Phase	Vibrational Focus	Desired State
1. Connection & Cleansing	The Family Tree	Sense of global connection and light.
2. Release of Charges	Releasing weights	Lightening of shoulders, freer breathing.
3. Repair & Harmony	Repairing bonds	Sense of peace, end of inner tensions.
4. Protection & Integrity	Sovereignty	Sense of security and independence.

C. 31. PROTOCOL: Harmonization of the Vibrational Field

(Healing through the Vibrational Transition of body and consciousness)

Harmonizing the vibrational field is the ultimate step that stabilizes all previous treatments. It ensures that the frequencies of the physical body and the subtle bodies sing the same melody of health and peace. The practitioner operates through **Vibrational Transition**: using their own sensation as a radar to smooth out the final rough edges of the aura and unify the global radiance.

1. OBJECTIVE AND PREPARATION

- **Objective:** Harmonize the entire vibrational field and stabilize the energetic bodies after a treatment or a period of imbalance.
- **Conditioning:** Settle into a stable posture. Breathe with the intention of becoming "unified."
- **Vibrational Intention:** *"I harmonize my vibrational field in unity and fluidity. I am in perfect coherence with my source frequency."*

2. THE DEPLOYED PROTOCOL (TRANSITION STEPS)

1. **Harmonization**
    - **Technique:** Focus your attention on the space between your cells and your auric field (the global vibrational space).
    - **Vibrational Movement:** Visualize waves of soft light circulating fluidly and harmoniously throughout your entire being.
    - **The Word:** *"I harmonize all my frequencies. May every part of my being vibrate in perfect consonance."*
2. **Balancing**
    - **Technique:** Feel the weight of your energy. Is it too high (head) or too low (feet)? Too far left or right?
    - **Vibrational Movement:** Gently bring all your attention back to your center of gravity (below the navel) to rebalance everything.
    - **The Word:** *"I rebalance my vibrational field. I find my center and my stability."*
3. **Alignment**
    - **Technique:** Straighten your spine through thought.
    - **Vibrational Movement:** Imagine an axis of pure light crossing your body from top to bottom, aligning all your centers.
    - **The Word:** *"I align my subtle bodies with my divine axis. I am perfectly upright and centered."*
4. **Radiance**

- **Technique:** Feel your aura expanding gently to about one meter all around you.
- **Vibrational Movement:** Let your inner light shine effortlessly, like a sun at high noon.
- **The Word:** *"I radiate my original light. My vibrational field is pure, brilliant, and vast."*

3. SEALING AND CLOSURE

- **Validation Test:** Breathe and observe the quality of your inner silence. If you feel "vast and calm," the harmonization is complete.
- **Closure:** *"My vibrational field is harmonized and sealed. I remain in this frequency of peace. Thank you."*
- **Physical Action:** Stretch to embody this new frequency in your muscles and tissues. Drink water to anchor the information.

RECAP TABLE

Phase	Consciousness Movement	Vibrational Result
1. Harmony	Totality / Union	End of inner dissonances.
2. Balancing	Centering / Balance	Sensation of solidity and calm.
3. Alignment	Verticality / Axis	Sense of alignment and rightness.
4. Radiance	Expansion / Light	Increase in vibrational rate.

PRACTICE SUMMARY

- **Note:** In **Vibrational Transition**, harmonization is felt as a "global breath." It is the moment when you no longer feel boundaries between your physical body and your energy.

C. 32. PROTOCOL: Boosting the Vibrational Rate

(Healing through the Vibrational Transition of body and consciousness)

Boosting the vibrational rate involves increasing the rotation frequency of the energy particles that compose us. A high rate promotes health, mental clarity, and natural protection against low frequencies. The practitioner operates through **Vibrational Transition**: using intention as a particle accelerator and breath as fuel to raise their own vibrational signature, without any external tools.

1. OBJECTIVES AND PREPARATION

- **Objective:** Raise the global vibrational frequency, boost vitality, and strengthen luminous radiance.
- **Conditioning:** Preferably standing to favor vertical circulation. Unlock the knees. Breathe in a tonic and deep manner.
- **Vibrational Intention:** *"I raise my vibrational rate to its optimal frequency of light and life. I am energized and radiant."*

2. THE DEPLOYED PROTOCOL (TRANSITION STEPS)

1. **Activation of Vital Energy**
    - **Technique:** Focus your attention on your sacral center (below the navel).
    - **Vibrational Movement:** Imagine a fire or a dynamo activating. Feel the heat rising and spreading throughout your pelvis.
    - **The Word:** *"I activate my source of vital energy. I awaken the life force within me."*
2. **Cellular Dynamization**
    - **Technique:** Feel every cell of your body as a small electric battery.
    - **Vibrational Movement:** With each inhalation, imagine you are increasing the voltage. Feel a tingling or light "fizzy" sensation throughout your body (arms, legs, back).
    - **The Word:** *"I dynamize each of my cells. My frequency is rising now."*
3. **Expansion of Radiance**
    - **Technique:** Focus on your aura, all around you.
    - **Vibrational Movement:** Feel your energy field becoming vaster, denser, and brighter. Visualize waves of golden light escaping from your pores.
    - **The Word:** *"I radiate my light with power. My vibrational field is high and strong."*
4. **Stabilization in High Frequency**

- **Technique:** Bring your awareness to the top of your head and the soles of your feet simultaneously.
- **Vibrational Movement:** Stabilize this high vibration so it is not a passing "spike" but a new stable state of being.
- **The Word:** *"I stabilize this high frequency in all my structures. I am aligned with the light."*

3. SEALING AND INTEGRATION

- **Validation Test:** Breathe and evaluate your level of enthusiasm or inner vitality. If you feel "vibrant" and alert, the dynamization is successful.
- **Closure:** *"My vibrational rate is high and stable. All is accomplished."*
- **Physical Action:** Rub your hands vigorously together, then pass them over your face. Drink a large glass of water to fix this kinetic energy in your fluids.

SUMMARY TABLE

Phase	Inner Action	Vibrational Feeling
1. Activation	Focus on the sacral center	Warmth, power build-up.
2. Dynamization	Global cellular focus	Tingling, gentle "electric current."
3. Expansion	Focus on the aura	Sense of greatness and strength.
4. Stabilization	Focus on Heaven-Earth axis	Feeling of being "plugged in" and solid.

C. 33. PROTOCOL: Cleansing of Energy Implants

(Healing through the Vibrational Transition of body and consciousness)

(Removing limiting energy implants—programming, limitations, manipulations—present in the aura or subtle bodies)

Energy implants are limiting structures or programs (manipulations, control memories) lodged in the aura or subtle bodies. They act as brakes on the sovereignty of the being. This protocol aims to identify and dissolve them. The practitioner uses their consciousness as a light scalpel and their sovereign intention to neutralize and evacuate these intrusive frequencies.

1. OBJECTIVES AND PREPARATION

- **Objective:** Remove limiting energy implants and restore the full sovereignty of the being.
- **Conditioning:** Settle into a state of absolute presence. Feel your spine as an inflexible pillar of strength.
- **Vibrational Intention:** *"I decree the total liberation of my vibrational field. I remove and dissolve every implant, program, or limitation not aligned with my divine source."*

2. THE DEPLOYED PROTOCOL (TRANSITION STEPS)

1. **Identification and Localization**
    - **Technique:** Scan your body and aura with your consciousness.
    - **Vibrational Movement:** Locate zones of "cold," sensations of a "foreign body," or unusual pressure points (often at the neck, plexus, or behind the knees).
    - **The Word:** *"I bring to light every limiting structure present in my subtle bodies. I see what must be released."*
2. **Neutralization of Programs**
    - **Technique:** Focus your awareness on the identified point.
    - **Vibrational Movement:** Project a high-frequency vibration (like a high-pitched sound or an ultra-white light) onto the implant to break its energetic coding.
    - **The Word:** *"I neutralize the influence and the program of this implant. Its frequency is now dissolved."*
3. **Extraction and Liberation**
    - **Technique:** Use your exhalation to "push" the structure out of your auric field.
    - **Vibrational Movement:** Feel the space clear, as if a thorn were being removed from your energetic skin.

- **The Word:** *"I extract this limitation from my aura. I free myself from it totally and definitively."*
- **Sensation:** A sudden lightening, a feeling of "taking one's place back."

4. Restoration of Sovereignty

- **Technique:** Fill the space left empty with your own original light.
- **Vibrational Movement:** Diffuse your energy from your heart toward the freed zone so that no imprint remains.
- **The Word:** *"I reintegrate my full power. I am the sole master of my energy field."*

5. Sealing and Protection

- **Technique:** Visualize a golden light membrane sealing your aura in a perfectly smooth manner.
- **The Word:** *"I seal my integrity. My field is protected and pure."*

3. SEALING AND INTEGRATION

- **Validation Test:** Pass your awareness over the area again. It should feel fluid and fully "belong" to your body.
- **Closure:** *"All is accomplished in rightness and light. I am free. Thank you."*
- **Physical Action:** Drink pure water. It is recommended to take a shower or a salt bath after this protocol to help evacuate vibrational residues.

SUMMARY TABLE

Phase	Consciousness Action	Vibrational State
1. Identification	Fine sensory scan	Detection of dissonances.
2. Neutralization	Disruptive vibration	Neutralization of the object.
3. Liberation	Evacuating exhalation	Exit from the golden field.
4. Sovereignty	Expansion of the Self	Sovereignty and wholeness.

📝 C. 34. PROTOCOL: Matrix Realignment Care

(Healing through the Vibrational Transition of body and consciousness)

The matrix is the geometric and vibrational framework that supports our existence. Matrix realignment allows the being to be placed back into its original "grid of perfection," erasing distortions accumulated from shocks and external influences. The practitioner operates through **Vibrational Transition**: using consciousness as a golden thread to reweave and realign their own energy framework with the Divine Matrix, without any external tools.

1. OBJECTIVES AND PREPARATION

- **Objective:** Realign all energy structures with the original matrix of perfection and health.
- **Conditioning:** Lie down or sit in a posture of total receptivity. Breathe with great fluidity.
- **Vibrational Intention:** *"I realign myself with my original matrix. I restore divine perfection in all layers of my being."*

2. THE DEPLOYED PROTOCOL (TRANSITION STEPS)

1. **Connection to the Matrix**
    - **Technique:** Focus your attention on the subtle geometric structure surrounding your body (like a cocoon of light lines).
    - **Vibrational Movement:** Feel the points of contact between your physical body and this light framework.
    - **The Word:** *"I activate my connection to the Sacred Matrix. I recognize my original light framework."*
2. **Identification of Distortions**
    - **Technique:** Scan your field to spot areas where the "weave" seems distorted, loose, or tangled.
    - **Vibrational Movement:** Breathe into these distortion zones with the intention of bringing back order and geometry.
    - **The Word:** *"I bring to light and I repair all distortions in my personal matrix."*
3. **Frequency Realignment**
    - **Technique:** Imagine a flow of crystalline light circulating through all the channels of your matrix.
    - **Vibrational Movement:** Feel every "thread" of your being tighten with rightness, creating a vibration of absolute coherence.
    - **The Word:** *"I align my structure with the frequency of divine perfection. Everything falls back into place according to the sacred order."*

- **Sensation:** A sense of rightness, as if everything finally "clicks" into place.

4. **Unification with the Source**
    - **Technique:** Visualize your personal matrix merging and harmonizing with the Universal Matrix (the Source).
    - **Vibrational Movement:** Feel that you are no longer a separate entity, but an integral and vibrant part of the Great Whole.
    - **The Word:** *"I am One with the Matrix of Life. My energy is pure, aligned, and infinite."*

5. **Sealing and Stabilization**
    - **Technique:** Visualize the realigned structure becoming set in a protective golden light.
    - **The Word:** *"I seal this matrix realignment. My structure is stable, coherent, and protected."*

3. SEALING AND INTEGRATION

- **Validation Test:** Breathe deeply and ask yourself: *"Is my structure aligned?"* You should feel a quiet strength and great inner clarity.
- **Closure:** *"The matrix realignment is accomplished. I thank the Source and my own consciousness."*
- **Physical Action:** Drink a glass of pure water to help your physical body embrace this new geometric structure. Move gently to feel your new verticality.

SUMMARY TABLE

Phase	Consciousness Focus	Transition State
1. Matrix	Geometric structure	Recognition of the light "Cocoon."
2. Distortions	Repairing the threads	End of distortions and leaks.
3. Realignment	Axial alignment	Sensation of order and rightness.
4. One	Unity with the All	Sense of peace and belonging.

📝 C. 35. PROTOCOL: Conscious Vibrational Protection

(Healing through the Vibrational Transition of body and consciousness)

Vibrational protection is not a rigid armor, but a resonance frequency that only allows in what is aligned with the Light. It prevents energy vampirism and pollution from surrounding emotions. The practitioner operates through **Vibrational Transition**: using their own will and breath to inform their aura and create an intelligent and sovereign protective membrane.

1. OBJECTIVE AND PREPARATION

- **Objective:** Create and stabilize a conscious protective field around the body and aura.
- **Conditioning:** Settle into a posture of quiet strength. Breathe deeply to occupy the entire space of your physical body.
- **Vibrational Intention:** *"I create an inviolable vibrational protection around my being. Only Love and Light may enter and exit."*

2. THE DEPLOYED PROTOCOL (TRANSITION STEPS)

1. **Centering and Alignment**
    - **Technique:** Focus your attention on your central axis, from crown to base.
    - **Vibrational Movement:** Feel this axis becoming a solid and brilliant pillar of light.
    - **The Word:** *"I am centered and aligned. My strength comes from my center."*
2. **Preliminary Cleansing**
    - **Technique:** Before sealing the protection, sweep your field with your breath.
    - **Vibrational Movement:** Expel any residual or foreign energy out of your personal space.
    - **The Word:** *"I cleanse my sacred space. Everything that is not mine leaves my field now."*
3. **Creation of the Light Membrane**
    - **Technique:** Visualize a sphere of golden or pearly white light about one meter all around you.
    - **Vibrational Movement:** Feel this boundary become dense and vibrant. Imagine this membrane is alive and conscious.
    - **The Word:** *"I activate my conscious protective shield. I am in total safety within my own radiance."*
4. **Impregnation of Divine Will**

- **Technique:** Focus on your solar plexus (the seat of will).
- **Vibrational Movement:** Diffuse a blue or gold force throughout the protective membrane.
- **The Word:** *"My will is law in my space. I refuse any unauthorized vibrational intrusion."*

5. **Final Sealing**

- **Technique:** Visualize a symbol of peace or light (like a sparkling point) sealing the membrane at the heart and head levels.
- **The Word:** *"I seal my protection in the Divine Light. It is accomplished."*

3. SEALING AND INTEGRATION

- **Validation Test:** Breathe and feel the space around you. You should feel "at home," in a cocoon of safety and clarity.
- **Closure:** *"I walk in the world, protected and radiant. Thank you."*
- **Physical Action:** Cross your arms over your chest for a moment to affirm your energy territory. Drink a glass of water to anchor this structure in your cells.

SUMMARY TABLE

Phase	**Inner Movement**	**Desired Vibrational State**
1. Centering/Alignment	Focus on central axis	Stability and presence.
2. Cleansing	Cleansing exhalation	Purity of the internal field.
3. Protection	Spherical expansion	Sense of safety and healthy boundaries.
4. Impregnation	Plexus affirmation	Sovereignty and protective strength.

C. 36. PROTOCOL: Deep Energetic Recharging

(Healing through the Vibrational Transition of body and consciousness)

Deep energetic recharging is necessary when vital reserves are exhausted by stress, illness, or overwork. Unlike a simple dynamization, this treatment acts as a "light IV drip" to restore internal batteries. The practitioner operates through **Vibrational Transition**: they become a conscious receptacle, opening their channels to draw energy directly from the universal Source and condense it into their vital centers, without any external tools.

1. OBJECTIVES AND PREPARATION

- **Objective:** Restore vital energy reserves, fill energetic voids, and nourish organs deeply.
- **Conditioning:** Lie down or sit with back support. Release all tension. Breathe slowly to lower the heart rate.
- **Vibrational Intention:** *"I open myself to the infinite flow of Life. I recharge my being deeply with the pure energy of the Source."*

2. THE DEPLOYED PROTOCOL (TRANSITION STEPS)

1. **Opening the Reception Channels**
    - **Technique:** Focus your attention on the top of your head (crown) and the palms of your hands.
    - **Vibrational Movement:** Feel these areas become porous and receptive, opening like flowers to the sun.
    - **The Word:** *"I open my reception channels. I am ready to receive vital energy."*
2. **Absorption of Prana / Vital Flow**
    - **Technique:** Visualize a flow of crystalline light descending from the sky and entering through your crown.
    - **Vibrational Movement:** With each inhalation, draw in this flow. Feel it pouring like warm nectar down your spine.
    - **The Word:** *"The flow of life pours into me. I nourish myself with universal light."*
3. **Filling Vital Reservoirs**
    - **Technique:** Focus on your three main centers: the belly (Hara), the heart, and the head.
    - **Vibrational Movement:** Feel these areas fill and densify. Imagine filling cups with a golden, luminous liqueur.
    - **The Word:** *"I fill my energy reservoirs. My vitality is restored in each center."*

- **Sensation:** A sense of fullness, pleasant weight, and internal warmth.

4. Cellular and Organic Irrigation

- **Technique:** Direct the accumulated energy toward tired organs or the entire nervous system.
- **Vibrational Movement:** Feel the energy seep into the smallest corners of your tissues, like thirsty soil absorbing rain.
- **The Word:** *"I nourish my cells and organs. Every fiber of my being is regenerated."*

5. Sealing the Reserve

- **Technique:** Visualize a thin film of protective light around your internal reservoirs to prevent loss.
- **The Word:** *"I seal this energy within me. It sustains me and dwells within me durably."*

3. SEALING AND INTEGRATION

- **Validation Test:** Ask yourself: *"Is my energy level restored?"* You should feel a quiet strength and deep calm, without the restlessness of simple excitement.
- **Closure:** *"I am recharged and strong. Thank you to the Source of Life. All is accomplished."*
- **Physical Action:** Remain still for a few minutes. Drink water and eat something light to anchor the energy in matter.

SUMMARY TABLE

Phase	Consciousness Action	Desired Vibrational State
1. Opening	Crown/palms opening	Tingling or coolness.
2. Absorption	Luminous breathing	Constant descending flow.
3. Filling	Focus on belly and heart	Density and fullness.
4. Irrigation	Internal diffusion	Diffuse warmth, deep soothing.

📝 C. 37. PROTOCOL: Complete Abundance Activation

(Healing through the Vibrational Transition of body and consciousness)

Abundance is a natural frequency of fullness, openness to life, and inner and outer prosperity. This protocol aims to return the being to its original vibration of fluidity by dissolving memories of lack and patterns of closure. The practitioner operates through **Vibrational Transition**: becoming the conscious vector of this energy by using their own body as a channel between Heaven and Earth.

1. PREPARATION AND CONNECTION

- **Grounding:** Feet connected to the Earth. *"I am grounded in the Earth, stable, present, available."*
- **Heart Centering:** Feel the heart illuminate. *"I open myself to the vibration of love and abundance."*
- **Vibrational Intention:** *"I am a conscious channel of Light and Universal Abundance. I connect to my original frequency of abundance and fluidity."*

2. THE DEPLOYED PROTOCOL (TRANSITION STEPS)

1. **Release of Blockages**
    - **Technique:** Focus on the pelvis and belly (security/reception).
    - **Vibrational Movement:** Exhale away fears of lack and limitations.
    - **The Word:** *"I let go of everything that blocks the circulation of Life. I release fears, memories of lack, and patterns of closure."*
2. **Conscious Vibrational Transition**
    - **Technique:** Focus on the energetic heart (inner sun).
    - **Vibrational Movement:** On the exhale, let the heart radiate a golden wave through your entire field.
    - **The Word:** *"I cross the vibrational gate. I choose the frequency of abundance, here and now. I allow my being to shift to its original vibration."*
3. **Re-information and Amplification**
    - **Technique:** Visualize the golden vibration in the heart (gratitude), belly (materialization), and head (confidence).
    - **The Word:** *"I am abundance. I receive, I create, I share. The energy of Life flows freely in me."*
4. **Stabilization and Grounding in Matter**
    - **Technique:** Feel the golden light descend from the heart to the feet and into the Earth.
    - **Vibrational Movement:** Visualize roots charging with light to fix the vibration in the physical.
    - **The Word:** *"I anchor the vibration of abundance in matter. It expresses itself in my life, my relationships, and my creations."*

3. CLOSURE AND INTEGRATION

- **Gratitude:** Thank Life and the body.
- **Physical Action:** Drink pure water and walk to return to ordinary consciousness.
- **Final Affirmation:** *"I give thanks to Life. I am aligned, abundant, and at peace."*

SUMMARY TABLE

Step	Energetic Movement	Vibrational Intention
1. Preparation	Grounding/Heart opening	I am a channel of Life.
2. Release	Dissolving blockages	I allow liberation.
3. Transition	Conscious shift (golden wave)	I choose abundance.
4. Re-info	Heart-belly-head activation	I radiate fluidity.
5. Stabilization	Material/Root anchoring	I embody abundance.

C. 38. PROTOCOL: Stimulation of Intuition

(Healing through the Vibrational Transition of body and consciousness)

Stimulating intuition consists of refining the connection with the Higher Self and opening the channels of subtle perception (clairvoyance, clairsentience). This protocol aims to dissolve mental "noise" to make room for inner guidance. The practitioner operates through **Vibrational Transition**: using their consciousness as a slider to activate perception centers (3rd eye, heart, crown) and harmonize the reception of messages, without any external tools.

1. OBJECTIVES AND PREPARATION

- **Objectives:**
    - Activate the connection to inner guidance.
    - Awaken subtle perceptions and clarity.
    - Dissolve mental blockages and doubts.
- **Conditioning:** Settle in a quiet place, close your eyes. Breathe slowly to soothe the mind.
- **Vibrational Intention:** *"I connect to my Higher Self. I strengthen my intuition and I open myself to receive clear and pure messages from my inner being."*

2. THE DEPLOYED PROTOCOL (TRANSITION STEPS)

1. **Cleansing Mental Resistances**
    - **Technique:** Focus on your forehead (3rd eye) and your temples.
    - **Vibrational Movement:** Imagine a cool breeze sweeping away parasitic thoughts, stress, and doubts.
    - **The Word:** *"I cleanse my mind of all clutter. I release resistances to my own guidance."*
2. **Release and Opening of Channels**
    - **Technique:** Focus on the top of your head (crown) and your heart.
    - **Vibrational Movement:** Feel these two centers open like chalices. Imagine a channel of light connecting your heart to the top of your skull.
    - **The Word:** *"I release my perception channels. I am fully open to receiving the messages of my soul."*
3. **Balancing and Clarity**
    - **Technique:** Focus on the center of your brain (pineal gland).
    - **Vibrational Movement:** Establish a vibration of calm and absolute transparency. Visualize a crystalline light purifying your inner vision.
    - **The Word:** *"I balance my perception centers. My inner vision is clear and without distortion."*

4. Connection and Discernment

- **Technique:** Feel the link between your 3rd eye and your heart.
- **Vibrational Movement:** Let the information flow freely. Feel the resonance between what you "see" or "hear" and what you "feel" in your heart.
- **The Word:** *"I am connected to my divine wisdom. I discern with accuracy the truth of my being."*

5. Confidence in Guidance

- **Technique:** Place your hands on your solar plexus (the seat of certainty).
- **Vibrational Movement:** Feel a solid warmth settle in, validating your perceptions.
- **The Word:** *"I have total confidence in my intuition. I let myself be guided by my inner light."*

3. SEALING AND INTEGRATION

- **Validation Test:** Ask yourself a simple question and observe the first sensation, image, or thought that emerges without analysis.
- **Closure:** *"My inner guidance is awakened and active. All is accomplished. Thank you."*
- **Physical Action:** Note your feelings or visions in a journal immediately. Drink pure water to fix the activation in your cells.

SUMMARY TABLE

Phase	Transition Zone	Desired State
1. Cleansing	Forehead / Temples	Mental silence, empty space.
2. Release	Crown / Heart	Receptivity and expansion.
3. Balancing	Pineal Gland	Transparency, crystalline clarity.
4. Confidence	Plexus / Heart	Inner certainty, end of doubt.

📝 C. 39. PROTOCOL: Activation of Spiritual Vision

(Healing through the Vibrational Transition of body and consciousness)

The activation of spiritual vision allows the material veil to be lifted to perceive subtle realities and access clairvoyance. This protocol aims to purify and open the center of inner vision. The practitioner operates through **Vibrational Transition**: using their own frequency as a key to unlock the third eye and align their perceptions with divine truth through breath and pure intention.

1. OBJECTIVE AND PREPARATION

- **Objective:** Activate spiritual vision, clairvoyance, and the ability to perceive beyond the material veil.
- **Conditioning:** Conscious breathing and deep mental relaxation in absolute calm.
- **Initial Test:** Ask internally: *"Can I activate my spiritual vision today?"* Wait for a feeling of opening.
- **Vibrational Intention:** *"I activate my spiritual vision in total safety. I open my third eye to perceive the truth beyond the material world, for my highest good and that of all."*

2. THE DEPLOYED PROTOCOL (TRANSITION STEPS)

1. **Purification and Opening**
    - **Technique:** Focus on the center of the forehead (3rd eye) and the top of the head.
    - **Vibrational Movement:** Visualize a sparkling white light purifying these centers of all opacity.
    - **The Word:** *"I purify my field of perception. Divine light dissolves all veils."*
2. **Release of Veils and Fears**
    - **Technique:** Focus on the back of your skull (occipital/image processing center).
    - **Vibrational Movement:** Feel the memories of fears related to "seeing" (past lives, traumas) evaporate with each exhale.
    - **The Word:** *"I release all fears and limiting beliefs that block my spiritual vision. I choose to see."*
3. **Activation of Clairvoyance**
    - **Technique:** Imagine a beam of indigo blue or violet light shooting from your forehead toward the infinite.
    - **Vibrational Movement:** Feel a gentle vibration or a slight tingling between your eyebrows.

- **The Word:** *"I activate my clairvoyance and my ability to perceive subtle planes. My vision is accurate and aligned."*

4. Alignment through the Heart

- **Technique:** Connect your 3rd eye to your heart with a thread of light.
- **Vibrational Movement:** Soften your vision with the frequency of love. Vision must be guided by compassion, not ego.
- **The Word:** *"I see through the eyes of my heart. My vision is imbued with love and wisdom."*

5. Protection of Vision

- **Technique:** Visualize a golden light membrane sealing your perception centers.
- **The Word:** *"I protect and seal my spiritual vision in the light. I only perceive what is right and divine."*

3. SEALING AND INTEGRATION

- **Restoration:** *"Spiritual vision is activated and protected in light, love, and truth. May this ability always serve wisdom and evolution."*
- **Grounding:** Imagine your feet taking deep root in the earth to bring perceptions into your physical incarnation.
- **Closure:** *"All is accomplished. I return fully to my body, enriched by this new clarity."*

SUMMARY TABLE

Phase	Transition Zone	Desired State
1. Purification	Frontal / Crown	Transparency and brilliance.
2. Release	Occiput / Neck	Lightening, end of apprehension.
3. Activation	Third Eye	Pulsation, expanded vision.
4. Alignment	Heart-Forehead Axis	Accuracy and compassion.
5. Sealing	Upper Aura	Security and stability of perceptions.

📝 C. 40. PROTOCOL: Activation of the Causal Chakra

(Healing through the Vibrational Transition of body and consciousness)

(Activating and opening the causal chakra (at the back of the head) for connection to higher planes and integration of the soul mission)

The causal chakra (located at the back of the head) is the center of higher guidance, the portal through which the soul receives instructions regarding its divine mission. Its activation allows for increased spiritual clarity and better integration of subtle planes into the physical incarnation. The practitioner operates through **Vibrational Transition**: using breath and presence to open this bridge between the soul and divine consciousness, facilitating the shift from a state of separation to a state of total connection.

1. PREPARATION AND OPENING

- **Conditioning:** Sit comfortably or stand with your back straight. Close your eyes.
- **Targeted Breathing:** Inhale white light through the crown. Exhale and release all tension in the nape and neck. Feel your breath settling at the back of the skull.
- **Vibrational Intention:** *"I activate my causal chakra to receive divine guidance and soul inspiration. I open myself to the purest frequency of guidance."*

2. THE DEPLOYED PROTOCOL (TRANSITION STEPS)

1. **Localization and Awakening**
    - **Technique:** Focus your attention precisely on the area at the back of the head (a few centimeters above the nape).
    - **Vibrational Movement:** Visualize a white or bluish luminous sphere beginning to pulse gently.
    - **The Word:** *"I become aware of my causal center. I activate this portal of light."*
2. **Opening Toward the Source**
    - **Technique:** Imagine this sphere opening like a lotus or expanding backward, creating a connection with the cosmos.
    - **Vibrational Movement:** Feel a golden ascending spiral rising from this area.
    - **The Word:** *"I open my consciousness to the higher planes. I deploy my spiritual antenna."*
3. **Connection and Alignment**
    - **Technique:** Mentally trace a fluid channel of light between your causal chakra, your third eye, and your heart.

- **Vibrational Movement:** Feel the circulation become vertical and effortless.
- **The Word:** *"I am connected to my soul mission. Guidance flows from my causal center to my heart."*

4. **Integration of Guidance**

- **Technique:** Place one hand on your heart and the other on the back of your neck.
- **Vibrational Movement:** Breathe deeply, feeling the spiritual information descend into your cells and physical body.
- **The Word:** *"I integrate the wisdom of my soul. My incarnated consciousness is now guided."*

3. SEALING AND INTEGRATION

- **Validation Test:** Feel your grounding and presence. If you experience deep calm and a sense of "clarity" behind the head, the activation is sealed.
- **Closure:** *"I thank the Divine Light and my higher consciousness. I seal this care in Love and Light. All is accomplished."*
- **Physical Action:** Drink pure water. Gently stretch the neck and shoulders. Note any perceived feelings or intuitive messages.

SUMMARY TABLE

Phase	**Consciousness Movement**	**Vibrational Effect**
1. Localization	Focus on back of skull	Awareness of the causal center.
2. Activation	Ascending golden spiral	Awakening of flow and expansion.
3. Connection	Vertical heart-head channel	Direct link with the Source.
4. Integration	Heart hand / Nape hand	Descent of guidance into the body.

C. 41. PROTOCOL: Activation of the Alta Major Chakra

(Healing through the Vibrational Transition of body and consciousness)

(Activating the Alta Major chakra (at the hollow of the nape) to develop subtle perceptions, clairvoyance, and higher intuition)

The Alta Major chakra (located at the base of the skull, in the hollow of the nape) is considered the "Portal of the Gods." It is the center that governs subtle perceptions, clairvoyance, and higher intuition by linking the heart to the pineal gland. The practitioner operates through **Vibrational Transition**: using breath and presence to fluidify this energetic passage, allowing for the union between human consciousness and divine guidance.

1. PREPARATION AND OPENING

- **Conditioning:** Sit or stand with a well-aligned back, head free, and nape relaxed. Gently close your eyes.
- **Targeted Breathing:**
  - *Inhale:* Feel the air rise along the spine to the nape.
  - *Exhale:* Let tension descend, as if opening a space of softness at the base of the skull.
- **Vibrational Intention:** Place your right hand at the base of the neck and the left on your heart. *"I activate my Alta Major chakra to receive light and divine guidance."*

2. THE DEPLOYED PROTOCOL (TRANSITION STEPS)

1. **Localization and Awakening**
   - **Technique:** Visualize a soft indigo-blue sphere at the base of the skull.
   - **Vibrational Movement:** Feel this sphere pulsing slowly like a luminous heart.
   - **The Word:** *"I become aware of my Alta Major center. I activate this portal of perception."*
2. **Opening of the Portal**
   - **Technique:** Imagine this sphere widening and becoming a channel of crystalline light.
   - **Vibrational Movement:** Feel an expansion both backward and vertically. The passage between your head and shoulders becomes vast.
   - **The Word:** *"I open my spiritual portal. I allow the circulation of pure vision."*
3. **Activation of the Flow**

- **Technique:** Visualize a golden ascending spiral starting from the nape and rising toward the top of the skull.
- **Vibrational Movement:** Feel the movement of energy activating your faculties of clairvoyance and inner listening.
- **The Word:** *"I activate my subtle perceptions. My higher intuition awakens now."*

4. **Connection and Alignment**

- **Technique:** Trace a vertical link between your heart, your nape (Alta Major), and your crown.
- **Vibrational Movement:** Feel the luminous flow circulate unhindered between these three points.
- **The Word:** *"I am connected to my guidance. My vision is aligned with the truth of my soul."*

3. SEALING AND INTEGRATION

- **Validation Test:** Breathe the following affirmation: *"I am guided by the light. I see with clarity and confidence."*
- **Closure:** *"I thank the Divine Light and my higher consciousness. I seal this care in peace and light."*
- **Protection:** Visualize a blue and gold luminous cloak resting on your shoulders, protecting your light channel.

SUMMARY TABLE

Phase	Consciousness Movement	Vibrational Effect
1. Localization	Breathing at the base of skull	Activation of the energy center.
2. Alta Major	Backward and vertical expansion	Opening of the spiritual portal.
3. Activation	Ascending golden spiral	Awakening of circulation and vision.
4. Connection	Vertical heart–nape–crown link	Establishing a guidance channel.

📝 C. 42. PROTOCOL: Activation of the Intuition Channel

(Healing through the Vibrational Transition of body and consciousness)

(Activating the intuition channel linking the third eye to the heart and the Alta Major chakra, to receive clear guidance)

Activating the intuition channel allows for the connection of the third eye, the heart, and the Alta Major chakra. This care creates a vibrational bridge that facilitates the reception of clear and luminous guidance from the soul. The practitioner operates through **Vibrational Transition**: using breath and presence to align their centers of perception and feeling, becoming a pure and fluid receiver, without any external tools.

1. PREPARATION AND OPENING

- **Conditioning:** Sit or stand with a straight yet supple spine, head free. Close your eyes.
- **Alignment Breathing:**
    - *Inhale:* Feel the light enter through the top of the head and descend to the heart.
    - *Exhale:* Release all thoughts and mental tension.
    - Feel the breath creating a fluid internal rhythm, a breath between Heaven and Earth.
- **Vibrational Intention:** Place one hand on your heart and the other on your third eye (between the eyebrows). Pronounce with conviction: *"I activate my intuition channel in pure light."* Feel the subtle link between these two points gently ignite.

2. THE DEPLOYED PROTOCOL (TRANSITION STEPS)

1. **Preparation of the Field (Protection & Purification)**
    - **Technique:** Visualize a sphere of golden light enveloping you entirely (Protection). Then, breathe in white light to cleanse your mind (Purification).
    - **The Word:** *"I am protected in the light. My mental field is pure and available."*
2. **Alignment and Balance**
    - **Technique:** Feel a luminous vertical axis crossing your body. Calm your polarities internally.
    - **Vibrational Movement:** Feel the centering on your soul and the harmony setting in.
    - **The Word:** *"I align my vertical axis. I am in perfect balance."*
3. **Activation of the Channel**

- **Technique:** Visualize a link of silver light connecting your third eye, your heart, and the back of your neck (Alta Major).
- **Vibrational Movement:** Feel this triangle of light activate. The intuitive flow begins to circulate freely between these three poles.
- **The Word:** *"I activate my intuition channel. I allow the flow of guidance to circulate within me."*

4. **Clarity and Reception**

- **Technique:** Imagine a crystal of light at the center of your brain, making your perceptions limpid.
- **Vibrational Movement:** Visualize a golden spiral setting the energy in motion throughout the entire channel.
- **The Word:** *"My vision is clear. I receive the messages of my soul with clarity."*

3. SEALING AND INTEGRATION

- **Validation Test:** Remain for a few moments in silence. Observe if an image, a word, or a sensation of peace emerges. If you feel "unified," the channel is active.
- **Closure:** *"I am a channel of divine light, pure and clear. I integrate this activation in peace and balance. All is accomplished."*
- **Physical Action:** Drink a large glass of water. If needed, gently massage your nape (Alta Major) to help stabilize the energy flow. Note any images or messages received in your journal.

SUMMARY TABLE

Phase	Consciousness Movement	Vibrational Effect
1. Protection / Purification	Golden sphere and white breath	Safety and mental cleansing.
2. Alignment / Balance	Vertical axis and calm	Soul alignment and harmony.
3. Intuition	Silver heart-forehead-nape link	Awakening and opening of intuitive flow.
4. Clarity / Reception	Crystal and golden spiral	Pure reception and movement.

PRACTICE ADVICE

- **Frequency:** This session lasts about 20 to 25 minutes. Practice according to your feeling, 1 to 3 times per month, to keep your channel "clean" and reactive.

- **Training Note:** In **Vibrational Transition**, intuition is a muscle. This protocol does not force the answer; it prepares the "ground" so that information can descend without filters.
- **Precision:** If the mind becomes restless during the treatment, simply return to the sensation of the hand on the heart to stabilize the vibration.

C. PRACTICAL PLATES

📄 1. Practical Plate: Vibrational Reading

1. What is Vibrational Reading?

Vibrational reading is a process that allows for the analysis of the energetic state of a person, place, or situation through frequencies perceived directly by the practitioner's body and consciousness. It combines:

- **Bodily resonance** (the body's ability to feel frequency variations).
- **Clair-information** (direct reception of energetic data).
- **Intuitive interpretation** of variations in density, heat, or fluidity within the vibrational field.

2. Objectives of Vibrational Reading

- Detect blockages, pollutions, or imbalances through sensing.
- Identify emotional, karmic, or transgenerational burdens in resonance.
- Check the state of the chakras and aura via manual or visual scanning.
- Understand the origin of an issue (physical, emotional, spiritual).
- Guide the treatment and the choice of transition frequencies to activate.

3. Preparation before Reading (State of Presence)

- **Grounding and Centering:** Breathe deeply. Connect to Earth and Heaven. Become a neutral channel.
- **Intention:** *"I ask to perceive accurate and benevolent information for this vibrational reading. May my body be the faithful instrument of this perception."*
- **Energetic Protection:** Visualize a bubble of light around yourself and the subject to maintain total neutrality.

4. Reading Procedure (Transition through Sensing)

- **Step 1**: Measurement of Global Vibrational Rate

  Close your eyes and connect to the person's field. Evaluate the global "luminosity" or "density." Ask internally: *"What is the current level of vitality?"* Receive the information as a number, color, or a sensation of lightness.

- **Step 2**: Aura Analysis (Vibrational Scan)

  Move your hands (or consciousness) slowly around the body at various distances. Ask: *"Does the aura show leaks, breaches, or interference?"* Observe the sensations:

  - **Tingling / Fluid Heat:** Balance, healthy circulation.

    - **Cold / Density / Resistance:** Blockage, energy leak, or disturbance.
    - **Void / Hollow:** Deep fatigue or need for recharging.
- **Step 3**: Chakra Analysis

  Focus your attention successively on each energy center. Feel the movement:
    - **Expansion / Radiance:** Active and open chakra.
    - **Jerky Vibration / Contraction:** Cleansing needed or release in progress.
    - **Absence of Sensation / Inertia:** Blockage or closure.
- **Step 4**: Detection of Energetic Pollutions

  Inquire through your sensing or clair-information:
    - "Are there limiting memories or implants?"
    - "Are there toxic cords or karmic burdens?"

    Let the answer emerge as an inner obviousness or a specific tension point in your own body (mirror effect).
- **Step 5**: Identification of Necessary Transition Frequencies

  Ask: *"Which frequency or protocol is best suited to transmute this state?"* Let the name of a protocol or a specific vibration impose itself on your consciousness to structure the care.

5. Closing the Reading

- Thank the energies and your guidance for the information received.
- Note your observations (densities, cold zones, intuitive messages).
- Perform a sweeping gesture on your arms to release any perceived imprints.

📄 2. Practical Plate: The Chakras

(Names, Colors, Functions, and Keywords)

Chakra	Color	Body Zone	Main Functions	Keywords
1. Root	🔴 Red	Base of spine	Security, grounding, survival, instincts	Grounding – Stability – Vitality
2. Sacral	🟠 Orange	Lower abdomen	Creativity, sexuality, emotions	Creation – Pleasure – Fluidity
3. Solar Plexus	🟡 Yellow	Stomach, diaphragm	Personal power, will, self-assertion	Confidence – Will – Strength
4. Heart	💚 Green / Pink	Center of chest	Love, compassion, balance	Love – Harmony – Openness
5. Throat	🔵 Light Blue	Throat, vocal cords	Communication, expression, truth	Expression – Truth – Listening
6. Third Eye	🟣 Indigo	Forehead, between brows	Intuition, inner vision, wisdom	Intuition – Clarity – Vision
7. Crown	⚪ Violet / White	Top of skull	Spiritual connection, universal consciousness	Spirituality – Unity – Awakening

📄 3. Practical Plate: List of Requests and Invocations for Healing

(Approach through Vibrational Transition and the Creative Word)

The invocation is the expression of pure intention. In **Vibrational Transition**, the Word serves as a rudder to steer the energy and stabilize the shift from a frequency of imbalance to a frequency of harmony. Here are the standard formulas to be adapted according to your sensing.

1. Invocations for Opening and Connection

These formulas establish the channel and secure the vibrational space.

- **Call to the Source:** *"I request the presence and assistance of the Divine Light and my healing guides. May this space be purified and dedicated to healing."*
- **Connection to the Subject:** *"I connect to the vibrational field of [Name] with respect for their free will and for their highest good."*
- **Practitioner Alignment:** *"I am a pure, neutral, and loving channel. May the life energy flow through me with accuracy."*

2. Invocations for Release and Cleansing

To be used for dissolving burdens, memories, and pollutions.

- **Global Cleansing:** *"By the power of my consciousness, I request the immediate cleansing of all pollutions and stagnant energies in this vibrational field."*
- **Release of Memories:** *"I request the dissolution of limiting memories [transgenerational / karmic / emotional] related to this issue."*
- **Severing of Cords:** *"I decree the cutting and transmutation of all toxic cords or attachments not aligned with the Light."*

3. Specific Healing Requests

To direct the transition toward a state of repair.

- **Rebalancing of Centers:** *"I invoke the perfect harmonization and alignment of all chakras and subtle bodies of [Name]. May balance be restored."*
- **Matrix Restoration:** *"I request the repair of the energetic framework and the realignment with the original matrix of perfect health."*
- **Emotional Soothing:** *"May the frequency of Peace and Compassion flood this heart and soothe all past wounds."*

4. Invocations for Activation and Dynamization

To raise the vibrational rate and anchor the new frequency.

- **Frequency Elevation:** *"I now activate the raising of [Name]'s vibrational rate to its optimal frequency of vitality."*

- **Intuitive Opening:** *"May the channels of perception and intuition be activated in clarity and safety."*
- **Abundance Activation:** *"I invoke the flow of Universal Abundance to circulate freely in every cell and every aspect of [Name]'s life."*

5. Invocations for Sealing and Closure

To fix the healing over time and close the channels.

- **Protection and Sealing:** *"I seal this care in the Divine Light. May this new frequency be protected and maintained permanently."*
- **Gratitude:** *"Thank you for this accomplished transition. I give thanks to Life and the Universal Consciousness."*
- **Disconnection:** *"The care is complete. I now disconnect from this vibrational field. I return fully to my own space."*

🗋 4. Practical Plate: Graduation of Energetic Intensity (0 to 10)

(Evaluation tool through sensing and Vibrational Transition)

This plate is a tool for self-assessment and vibrational diagnosis. It allows you to subjectively but precisely quantify the level of vitality, the density of a blockage, or the effectiveness of a transmutation.

1. Understanding the 0 to 10 Scale

- **Vitality Rate:** 0 = total exhaustion / 10 = full luminous power.
- **Blockage Density:** 0 = total fluidity / 10 = absolute crystallization (pain or energy knot).
- **Stress/Emotion Intensity:** 0 = absolute peace / 10 = emotional overwhelm.

2. Definition of Frequency Levels

- **Level 0: Absence of Signal / Critical Void**
    - *Action:* Deep energetic recharging (Protocol C36) is imperative.
- **Levels 1 to 3: Low Intensity / State of Fragility**
    - *Sensing:* Marked fatigue, retracted aura, or diffuse "cold."
- **Levels 4 to 6: Moderate Intensity / State of Vigilance**
    - *Sensing:* Functional but unstable energy, localized tension, fluctuating emotions.
- **Levels 7 to 9: High Intensity / State of Crisis or Saturation**
    - *Sensing:* Sharp physical or emotional pain, "tight knot" feeling.
- **Level 10: Maximum Intensity / State of Fullness or Urgency**
    - *Sensing:* Maximum radiance (positive) or acute suffering/shock (negative).

3. Practical Use in a Session

1. **Initial Scan:** Connect and ask: *"On a scale of 0 to 10, what is the density of this blockage?"*
2. **Protocol Choice:** If density is 7/10, choose a release protocol. If vitality is 3/10, prioritize recharging.
3. **Measuring the Transition:** After each step, re-evaluate. Success is confirmed when the blockage drops toward 0 and vitality rises toward 8–10.

Summary Table for the Practitioner

Score	Energy State	Physical/Vibrational Feeling	Recommended Action
0-2	Deficiency	Cold, void, lack of radiance.	**Nourish** (Recharge)

Score	**Energy State**	**Physical/Vibrational Feeling**	**Recommended Action**
3-5	Imbalance	Heaviness, tingling, instability.	**Harmonize** (Balance)
6-8	Saturation	Excessive heat, tension, pain.	**Release** (Cleanse)
9-10	Paroxysm	Sensation of suffocation or ecstasy.	Anchor / Stabilize

🗋 5. Practical Plate: Healing Journal

(Vibrational Transition)

A complete and structured template for your **Session Journal**, specifically adapted to the Vibrational Transition method (direct work through the body and sensing, without tools).

User Note: This sheet is designed to document the process of shifting from one frequency state to another. It prioritizes the observation of bodily sensations, energetic flows, and consciousness shifts.

SESSION IDENTIFICATION

- **Date:** [DD/MM/YYYY]
- **Practitioner:** ________________________________
- **Subject / Client:** ________________________

1. INITIAL STATE (VIBRATIONAL ANAMNESIS)

Describe the starting frequency before any intervention.

- **Global bodily sensing:** (Tensions, empty zones, density, temperature)
- **Dominant emotional state:** ___________________________
- **Perceived frequency (Energy level):** ◯ Low | ◯ Neutral | ◯ High

2. ALIGNMENT AND GROUNDING PHASE

The use of the body as a channel.

- **Preferred grounding point:** (Feet, pelvis, abdominal breathing)
- **Quality of presence:** _________________________________
- **Observations:** (Yawning, chills, immediate sensation of heaviness or lightness)

3. VIBRATIONAL TRANSITION PROCESS

Description of the passage from one state to another (the "shift").

- **Active resonance zone:** (Where is the change felt first? Heart, plexus, hands, crown?)
- **Nature of the flow:** (Fine vibrations, circulating heat, tingling, expansion, spiral)
- **Obstacles encountered:** (Physical resistance, parasitic thoughts, emotional blockages)
- **Moment of the shift:** (Describe the precise instant the frequency changed state)

4. FINAL STATE (INTEGRATION)

Observation of the new stabilized frequency.

- **Sensation of "After":**_________________________________
- **Mental clarity:** (Soothed thoughts, clearer vision, inner silence)
- **Quality of bodily sensing:** (Fluidity, vertical alignment, sense of unity)

5. SUMMARY AND BODY MESSAGES

- **Evolution of perceived vibrational rate:**___________________
- **Key observations for follow-up:**_______________________
- **Post-session advice (Hydration, rest, grounding):** _________

6. Practical Plate: Duration and Frequency of Care

(Vibrational Transition)

Since this practice is based on pure sensing and biological adjustment, time management differs radically from classic energy healing.

User Note: Vibrational Transition does not obey a linear clock, but a biological and frequency-based one. This plate serves as a landmark to structure your sessions while respecting the ecology of the client's body.

1. DURATION OF A TYPICAL SESSION

Time is a vector of stabilization here. There is no point in prolonging if the shift has occurred.

- **Reception and Induction Phase (10 to 15 min):** Time needed to lower brain waves (shifting to Alpha/Theta) and establish the sensory connection between practitioner and client.
- **Core of the Transition (20 to 40 min):** The active sensing phase. Duration varies according to tissue resistance and the depth of the informational knot. Stop when the body manifests the "point of neutrality" (deep stillness or a sigh of relief).
- **Integration and Return Phase (10 min):** Essential quiet time for the new vibrational rate to imprint into cellular memory.

Golden Rule: In Vibrational Transition, "doing more" is not "doing better." Once the shift is felt and stabilized, the session is over.

2. FREQUENCY OF INTERVENTIONS

The body needs time to metabolize the change in frequency.

- **Crisis Care or Major Transition:**
  - **Rhythm**: 1 session every 7 to 10 days.
  - **Objective:** Support the nervous system during a shock or radical life change.
- **Foundational Work (Structural transformation):**
  - **Rhythm**: 1 session every 3 or 4 weeks (corresponding to the cellular renewal cycle).
  - **Objective:** Progressively align the physical body with new frequencies of consciousness.
- **Maintenance and Vibrational Hygiene**:
  - **Rhythm:** At each change of season or as needed.
  - **Objective:** Clearing energetic residue and realigning the axes of sensing.

3. INDICATORS FOR STOPPING OR REST

The practitioner must be attentive to signs of client saturation:

- **Sensory Saturation:** The client no longer feels anything or experiences sudden, irrepressible fatigue.
- **Energetic Rebound:** If the body manifests excessive involuntary movements (shaking), the session must move toward final grounding.
- **"Assimilation Window":** Always leave at least 72 hours between two different physical approaches (massage, osteopathy, etc.) to avoid blurring the vibrational message.

4. SELF-CARE AND PERSONAL PRACTICE

For the practitioner, the frequency of their own transition is daily.

- **Daily Alignment (5-10 min):** In the morning, to calibrate sensing.
- **Post-session Discharge:** Immediately after each session, use bodily sensing to evacuate the client's residual frequencies.

7. Practical Plate: Post-Session Reactions

(Integration and Adjustments)

This plate helps the practitioner anticipate and explain to the client the biological and vibrational readjustment phenomena that follow immediately or in the days after treatment.

User Note: Vibrational Transition triggers a process of self-regulation within the body. This document lists the classic manifestations of moving toward a new state of balance. It is recommended to discuss these points with the client at the end of the session.

1. THE RELEASE CRISIS (OR "HEALING CRISIS")

The shift from a low (crystallized) frequency to a fluid frequency can cause a temporary "cleansing."

- **Physical manifestations:** Muscle soreness without physical effort, fleeting headaches, increased intestinal transit, or mild skin symptoms.
- **Emotional manifestations:** Resurgence of old memories, a need to cry without an apparent reason, or temporary irritability.
- **Meaning:** The body is evacuating toxins (physical and informational) that were held by the old vibrational state. This is a sign that the transition has successfully occurred.

2. STATE OF DEEP FATIGUE

Cellular reorganization consumes a significant amount of metabolic energy.

- **The feeling:** A sensation of "heaviness," an immediate need for sleep, or a feeling of floating (shift in consciousness).
- **The explanation:** The parasympathetic nervous system takes over to integrate the new frequency parameters. The body "unplugs" the mind to prioritize internal repair.
- **Advice:** Restorative sleep and complete rest within the 12 hours following the treatment.

3. FLEETING EUPHORIA AND ENERGY SURGE

Conversely, lifting a blockage can release a massive charge of vital energy.

- **The feeling:** Sensation of lightness, increased mental clarity, a desire to take action, sudden disappearance of chronic pain.
- **The trap:** Wanting to use this energy immediately for exhausting tasks.
- **Advice:** Channel this vitality to stabilize the new state rather than dispersing it. Observe the inner calm rather than the excitement.

4. INTEGRATION PHASES (Chronology)

Time Elapsed	Vibrational Phase	Recommendations
0h - 6h	Shift Phase	Drink plenty of water; avoid screens and loud noises.
6h - 48h	Cleansing Phase	Welcome emotions; practice gentle walking; eat light meals.
3 - 7 days	Stabilization Phase	The new state becomes the "norm." Observe changes in behavior.

5. RECENTERING PROTOCOL (In case of strong reaction)

If the client feels too "open" or unstable after the session:

- **Physical grounding:** Walk barefoot on the ground, eat dense foods (root vegetables), or take a lukewarm shower visualizing the water washing away the surplus.
- **Box Breathing:** Practice 4 cycles of slow breathing to bring consciousness back into the bone structure.
- **Earth contact:** Touch wood or stones to discharge the static electricity generated by the transition.

🗋 8. Practical Plate: Stopping and Resuming a Care Session

(Mastery of the Flow)

A crucial aspect of Vibrational Transition: knowing how to interrupt the process if necessary and how to restart the flow without losing the established sensory connection.

User Note: In Vibrational Transition, continuity of sensing is key. However, external factors or physiological reactions may require a temporary suspension. This plate defines the protocol to "freeze" the vibrational state and restart it safely.

1. WHY INTERRUPT A SESSION?

The practitioner must discern when suspension is preferable to continuing.

- **Nervous system saturation:** The client shows signs of rejection (excessive agitation, prolonged apnea, cold sweats).
- **External interruption:** Sudden noise, intrusion, or environmental emergency breaking the field of presence.
- **Practitioner limits:** Loss of neutrality, sudden fatigue, or loss of direct sensing (disconnection).
- **Integration plateau:** The body requests a break to "digest" a first shift before starting the next.

2. THE MOMENTARY STOP PROTOCOL ("On Hold")

The goal is to avoid a brutal drop in frequency.

- **Progressive Withdrawal:** Do not remove your hands or attention abruptly. Decrease the intensity of your vibrational presence gently, like lowering the volume of a sound.
- **Safety Anchor:** Before breaking physical or visual contact, visualize the current frequency stabilizing in the client's pelvis.
- **Verbal Explanation:** Say in a calm voice: *"We are taking a short break to let the body integrate this level."* This reassures the mind and prevents a sudden exit from the altered state of consciousness.

3. THE RESUMPTION PROTOCOL ("Restarting the Flow")

How to find the exact frequency where it was left off.

- **Practitioner Realignment:** Before touching the client again, the practitioner must return to their own vertical axis and find their inner sensing.
- **Search for the Contact Point:** Reposition yourself on the last active resonance zone.
- **Vibrational Call:** Do not try to "push" the energy. Wait to feel the micro-movement or heat again before restarting the transition process.

- **Respiratory Synchronization:** Use a shared deep breath to re-establish the energetic bridge between you and the client.

4. WHEN TO PERMANENTLY END A SESSION?

- **The "Point of No Return":** If after two attempts to resume, the flow remains blocked or the client expresses extreme fatigue.
- **Early Accomplishment:** If the vibrational shift happened lightning-fast and the body displays profound, premature peace.
- **Closing Signal:** A sensation of absolute neutrality, as if the client's body has become "silent" to the practitioner's requests.

SUMMARY OF KEY GESTURES

Action	Technical Gesture	Mental Intention
Stop	Light pressure then slow withdrawal.	"Everything is safe, here and now."
Wait	Keep one hand at a distance from the body.	"The process continues autonomously."
Resumption	Gentle contact and breath sync.	"I reconnect to the present flow."

9. Practical Plate: Posture and Ergonomics for the Practitioner

(HOW TO POSITION YOUR BODY TO AVOID EXHAUSTION DURING TRANSMISSION)

In Vibrational Transition, the practitioner's body is both the measuring instrument and the transmission channel. Poor posture doesn't just lead to physical pain; it "scrambles" the signal and limits the effectiveness of the care.

User Note: For the frequency transition to be fluid, the practitioner's body must be a conductor without resistance. This plate details how to set yourself up to maintain high resonance without physical or energetic exhaustion.

1. THE FOUNDATIONS: GROUNDING

Vibrational transfer requires a stable base to avoid "drawing" from your own reserves.

- **Foot Position:** Feet shoulder-width apart, knees never locked (maintain a micro-flexion). This allows energy to flow without stagnating in the joints.
- **Weight Distribution:** Weight should be slightly forward (on the balls of the feet) for an active presence, or perfectly centered for neutral listening.
- **Earth Contact:** Imagine your legs are extensions of the ground. The "heavier" you are at the bottom, the "lighter" and more subtle you can be with your hands.

2. THE VERTICAL AXIS (THE CHANNEL'S SPINE)

The spinal column is the antenna that captures and transmits frequencies.

- **Neutral Pelvis:** Avoid excessive arching (hyperlordosis). A well-placed pelvis releases the diaphragm and allows for the deep breathing essential to the transition.
- **Crown of the Head:** Imagine a silk thread pulling you upward. This releases the cervical vertebrae and allows vibrational information to rise to the higher perception centers.
- **Shoulders and Elbows:** Shoulders must be low and relaxed. Keep elbows close to the body as much as possible to save muscular strength and prioritize sensitive transmission.

3. THE HANDS: BETWEEN LISTENING AND EMISSION

In this practice, the hand does not "massage," it "resonates."

- **The "Feather" Hand:** Contact should be firm but without pressure. A hand that is too tense becomes deaf to micro-vibrations.
- **Weight Transfer:** To apply a deeper presence, do not push with arm muscles. Lean your entire body forward from the ankles. It is your "body weight" acting, not your strength.

- **Alternation:** If a position becomes uncomfortable, change sides. Practitioner discomfort creates "pollution" in the vibrational field of the care session.

4. EFFORT MANAGEMENT AND RECOVERY

Warning Point	Risk for Practitioner	Ergonomic Solution
Reflex Apnea	Sudden fatigue and flow blockage.	Exhale consciously during strong transition phases.
Neck Tension	Headaches and loss of clarity.	Slightly tuck the chin toward the sternum.
Leaning on one leg	Energetic imbalance.	Practice the "cat walk" (fluid weight transfer from one leg to the other).

5. POSTURAL CLEANSING RITUAL

- **Shake the hands:** Gently shake hands and arms to release residual tension.
- **Field Break:** Cross your arms over your chest, then open them wide while inhaling to clearly mark the end of the care channel.
- **Water Wash:** Run cold water over your forearms to close energetic pores and bring consciousness back to the physical body.

🗋 10. Practical Plate: Daily Rituals

(Reading and Maintenance)

This plate is fundamental as it addresses the maintenance of the practitioner's primary instrument: themselves. It bridges with "Vibrational Reading" to ensure constant clarity of perception.

User Note: Vibrational Transition demands rigorous hygiene of consciousness. These rituals are not optional; they are the foundations necessary to refine sensory reading and preserve the practitioner's energetic integrity daily.

1. MORNING RITUAL: "TUNING THE INSTRUMENT"

- **Presence Scan (Internal Vibrational Reading):** Scan your body from bottom to top. Note zones of density, heat, or void. *Objective: Know your "background noise" so you don't confuse it with the client's frequencies later.*
- **Field Expansion:** Through breath, visualize your inner space expanding beyond the skin. Feel the boundary of your aura.
- **Axis Affirmation:** Visualize your spine as a channel of light. Mentally state: *"I am a pure, neutral, and stable channel."*

2. PRE-SESSION RITUAL: "ENTERING RESONANCE"

- **Symbolic Hand Wash:** Activate the sensory sensors in your palms with water or by rubbing them together.
- **Mental Void:** Practice 3 "sighing" breaths to evacuate personal concerns.
- **Sensory Opening:** Set the intention to listen with your whole body. Become a "giant ear."

3. POST-SESSION RITUAL: "THE DISCONNECTION"

- **Bridge Break:** Visualize the sensory links with the client dissolving. Return fully to your own physical envelope.
- **Earth Transfer:** Place hands on the ground or a stone wall for one minute to discharge excess static electricity.
- **Change of State:** Drink a glass of still water mindfully to rinse transition memories.

4. EVENING RITUAL: "SYNTHESIS AND CLEANSING"

- **Vibrational Recapitulation:** Briefly review the day's sessions. If a sensation persists (phantom pain, emotion), consciously exhale it.
- **Shower of Light:** Under a real shower or through visualization, let the water carry away all traces and frequencies that do not belong to you.

5. VIBRATIONAL MAINTENANCE TABLE

Frequency	Key Action	Benefit
Daily	Body Scan & Grounding	Clarity of sensory reading.
Weekly	Nature Immersion (Forest/Water)	Recharging etheric batteries.
Monthly	Receiving a session from another practitioner	Hygiene and humility of the channel.

11. Practical Plate: Express Practices

(2 to 10 minutes)

(Quick interventions using the Vibrational Transition method, allowing for immediate rebalancing through the body and consciousness in just a few minutes.)

In a practitioner's daily life or for an urgent need, it is sometimes necessary to modify a vibrational frequency in record time. These "Express" protocols rely on the intensity of presence and the precision of the Word. They allow for a shift from a state of disturbance to a state of stability without complex processes.

1. Flash Alignment (2 min)

To recenter before an appointment or after a minor shock.

- **Action:** Stand with feet firmly grounded.
- **Vibrational Movement:** Inhale a line of silver light that crosses your spine from top to bottom. Exhale, diffusing this light into your aura.
- **The Word:** *"Axis, Center, Alignment. I am here and now, fully present in my body."*
- **Result:** Immediate sensation of verticality and mental calm.

2. Emergency Cleansing - "Light Shower" (3 min)

After passing through a heavy location or a burdensome interaction.

- **Action:** Use your hands to sweep the space in front of you without touching the body.
- **Vibrational Movement:** Visualize a rain of violet and white sparks dissolving energetic dross on your vibrational "skin."
- **The Word:** *"I release and transmute all energy that does not belong to me. Immediate Nikkuy."*
- **Result:** Lightening of the weight on the shoulders and disappearance of sudden fatigue.

3. The Consciousness Shield (2 min)

To instantly protect yourself before entering a hostile environment.

- **Action:** Close your eyes and slightly contract the solar plexus.
- **Vibrational Movement:** Feel your radiance intensify and densify to form an inviolable golden membrane.
- **The Word:** *"(Protection). My light is my law. Only love passes through this field."*
- **Result:** Feeling of inner security and sovereignty.

4. "Flash" Recharge (5 min)

In case of a sudden drop in energy or a "slump."

- **Action:** Sit with hands open toward the sky.

- **Vibrational Movement:** Breathe through the top of the skull (Crown) and connect directly to the reservoir of the Source. Imagine a golden battery filling up in your lower abdomen.
- **The Word:** *"(Abundance of Life). I fill my reservoirs now."*
- **Result:** Regain of vitality and restored clarity of mind.

5. Emotional Harmonization (5 to 10 min)

To calm rising anger, fear, or anxiety.

- **Action:** Place one hand on the heart, the other on the forehead.
- **Vibrational Movement:** Circulate energy in a loop between your brain and your heart. Breathe into the emotional "knot" until it expands and evaporates.
- **The Word:** *"(Balance). Peace within me, Peace around me."*
- **Result:** Soothing of the heart rate and return to emotional calm.

SUMMARY OF EXPRESS COMMANDS

Need	Protocol	Duration	Key Word
Scattering	Alignment	2 min	Axis and Center
Pollution	Light Shower	3 min	Cleansing
Vulnerability	Shield	2 min	Protection
Exhaustion	Solar Flash	5 min	Abundance of life
Stress/Shock	Harmonization	7 min	Balance

Note for the Practitioner:

The effectiveness of an express practice depends on your vibrational faith. In **Vibrational Transition**, energy obeys clear intention. The more you practice these short modules, the more your system will respond instantaneously to the Word and the Sensing. These plates are ideal for maintaining your vibrational hygiene throughout the day without weighing down your schedule.

CONCLUSION OF THE APPENDIX

The Integration of the Inner Master

We have reached the end of this practical guide. The protocols, plates, and methods presented in these appendices are not mere recipes, but keys to passage. By closing this manual, you are not leaving a teaching behind; you are entering the living application of **Vibrational Transition**.

The Art of Absolute Simplicity

Vibrational Transition brings us back to the essentials: the body and consciousness. We have learned that the most sophisticated tool is not external to us, but resides in our capacity to feel, to name (the Word), and to choose our frequency. By renouncing physical tools, you have activated your inner technology. You have discovered that healing and alignment are not laborious processes, but immediate shifts in consciousness.

The Posture of Tomorrow's Practitioner

The practitioner of the new era is no longer the one who "repairs," but the one who witnesses and facilitates. Through your own centering, grounding, and clarity, you offer a space where the receiver's frequency can adjust through resonance. Your responsibility is not to carry the healing, but to maintain the vibration of the Solution until matter aligns with it.

Toward Sovereign Autonomy

The ultimate goal of this guide is your autonomy. Whether you use these protocols for yourself or for others, keep in mind that every session is an opportunity to strengthen your vibrational faith. Do not seek technical perfection; seek the accuracy of the feeling.

- **Remember:** Vibration precedes form.
- **Remember:** Your intention is the law of your field.
- **Remember:** The body never lies; it is your most faithful compass.

Closing Words

Vibrational Transition is a path of returning Home—to that inner space where everything is already harmony, abundance, and health. By using the tools in this guide, you participate in the elevation of collective consciousness, one shift at a time, one breath at a time.

May your practice be filled with joy, curiosity, and an unwavering trust in Life. You are now equipped to navigate the frequencies of the new paradigm.

Everything is accomplished. The path continues in Light, Love, and Presence.